MW00911802

125 SUPER SONGS OF THE SUPER STARS

SUPERS OF THE SUPERSTARS EASY GUITAR

C O N T

DON'T LET IT BRING YOU DOWN

Words and Music by
NEIL YOUNG

Slowly, in 2

Old man ly - in' by the side of the road___ with the
Blind man run - ning through the light of the night___ with an

lor - ries roll - ing by,___ blue moon sink - ing from the
an - swer in his hand,___ come on down to the

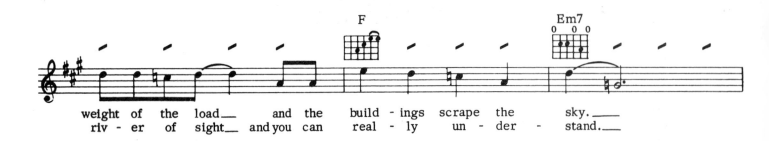

weight of the load___ and the build - ings scrape the sky.___
riv - er of sight___ and you can real - ly un - der - stand.___

Cold wind rip - ping down the al - ley at dawn___ and the morn - ing pa - per
Red lights flash - ing through the win - dow in the rain, can you hear the si - rens

flies, ___ dead man ly - ing by the side of the road___ with the
moan?___ White cane ly - ing in a gut - ter in the lane if you're

day - light in his eyes. }
walk - ing home a - lone. } Don't let it bring you down,___ it's

on - ly cas - tles burn - ing; find some - one who's turn - ing, and

you will come a - round.___

Don't let it bring you down, it's on - ly cas - tles

burn - ing; just find some - one who's turn - ing and

you will come a - round.___

BAD, BAD LEROY BROWN

Words and Music by
JIM CROCE

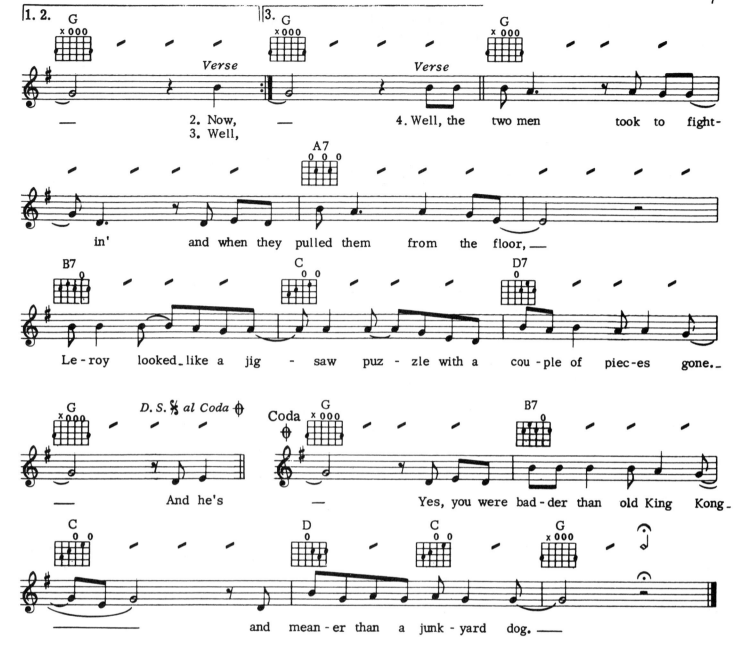

Additional lyrics

2. Now, Leroy, he a gambler, and he like his fancy clothes.
And he like to wave diamond rings in front of everybody's nose.
He got a custom Continental. He got a Eldorado too.
He got a thirty-two gun in his pocket for fun. He got a razor in his shoe.

   (Chorus)

3. Well, Friday, 'bout a week ago, Leroy shootin' dice.
And at the edge of the bar sat a girl name of Doris and oh, that girl looked nice.
Well, he cast his eyes upon her and the trouble soon began
And Leroy Brown, he learned a lesson 'bout messin' with the wife of a jealous man.

   (Chorus)

4. Well, the two men took to fightin' (etc.)

   (Chorus)

LADY DOWN ON LOVE

Words and Music by
RANDY OWEN

9

she's _____ a la - dy __ down _____ on

love. She _____ needs some - bod - y to

gen - tly pick her up. She's _____ got her

free - dom, but she'd rath - er __ be bound to a

man who would love her and nev - er let her down.

Now she's _____ a la - dy __

down _____ on ___ love.

WE ARE FAMILY

Words and Music by
NEIL RODGERS and BERNARD EDWARDS

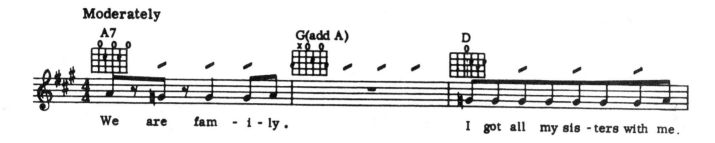

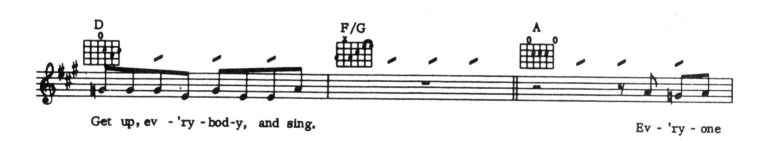

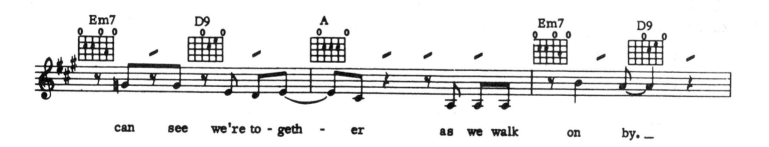

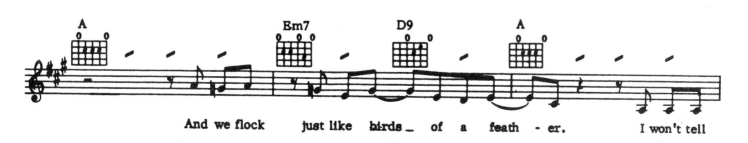

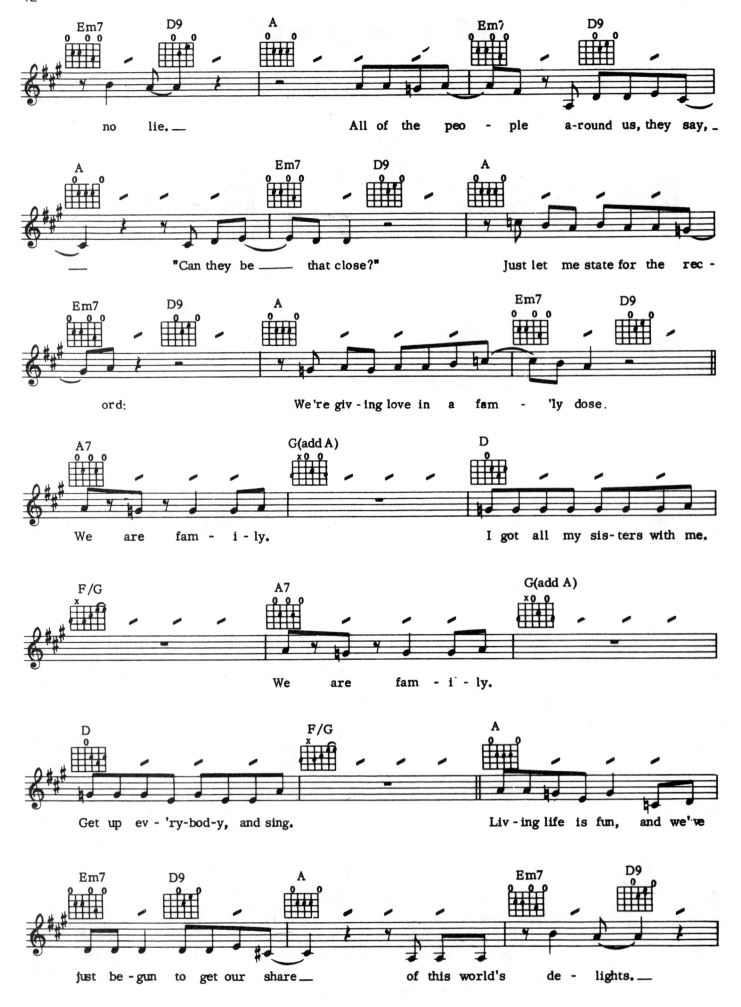

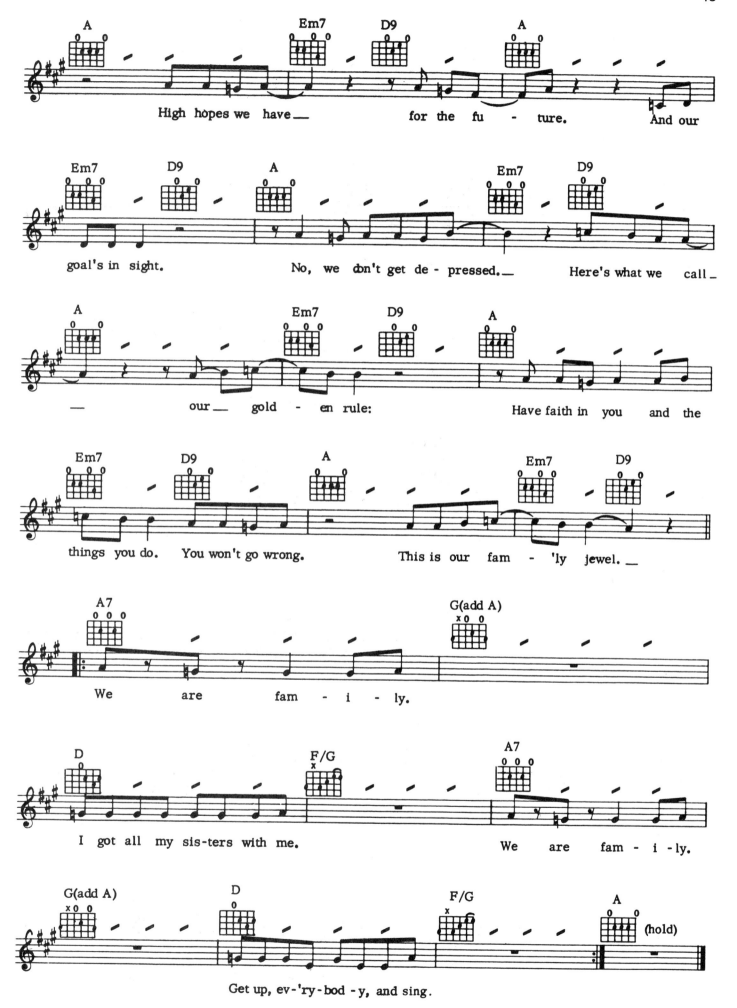

EVERGREEN
(Love Theme from "A STAR IS BORN")

Words by
PAUL WILLIAMS

Music by
BARBRA STREISAND

15

LISTEN TO THE MUSIC

Words and Music by
TOM JOHNSON

DA YA THINK I'M SEXY?

Words and Music by
ROD STEWART,
CARMINE APPICE and DUANE HITCHINGS

HOLLYWOOD NIGHTS

Words and Music by
BOB SEGER

Moderately bright Rock beat

Verse
1. She stood there, bright as the sun, on that Cal - i - for - nia coast.

He was a mid - west - ern boy on his own.

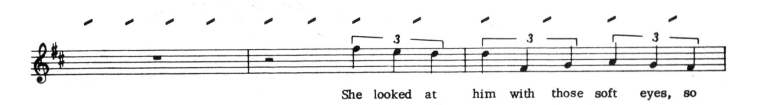

She looked at him with those soft eyes, so

in - no - cent ___ and blue. He knew right

then he was too far from home.

Chorus

And those Hol-

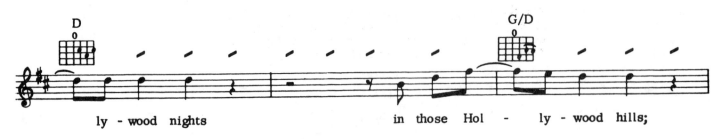

ly - wood nights   in those Hol - ly - wood hills;

she was look - ing so right   in her dia - monds and frills.

Oh, those big ___ cit - y nights ___   in those high, ___

___ roll - ing hills; ___   a - bove all the lights,

To Coda ⊕   *D. C. (with repeats) al Coda* ⊕   Coda

she had all ___ of her skills.

Additional lyrics

Verse 2. She took his hand and she led him along that golden beach.
They watched the waves tumble over the sand.
They drove for miles and miles up those twisting, turning roads.
Higher and higher and higher they climbed.

Chorus I. And those Hollywood nights (etc.)

Verse 3. He'd headed west 'cause he felt that a change would do him good.
See some old friends, good for the soul.
She had been born with a face that would let her get her way.
He saw that face and he lost all control.

Verse 4. Night after night and day after day it went on and on.
Then came that morning he woke up alone.
He spent all night staring down at the lights of L. A.,
Wondering if he could ever go home.

Chorus II. And those Hollywood nights in those Hollywood hills:
It was looking so right. It was giving him chills.
Oh, those big city nights in those high, rolling hills,
Above all the lights with a passion that kills.

PEACEFUL EASY FEELING

Words and Music by
JACK TEMPCHIN

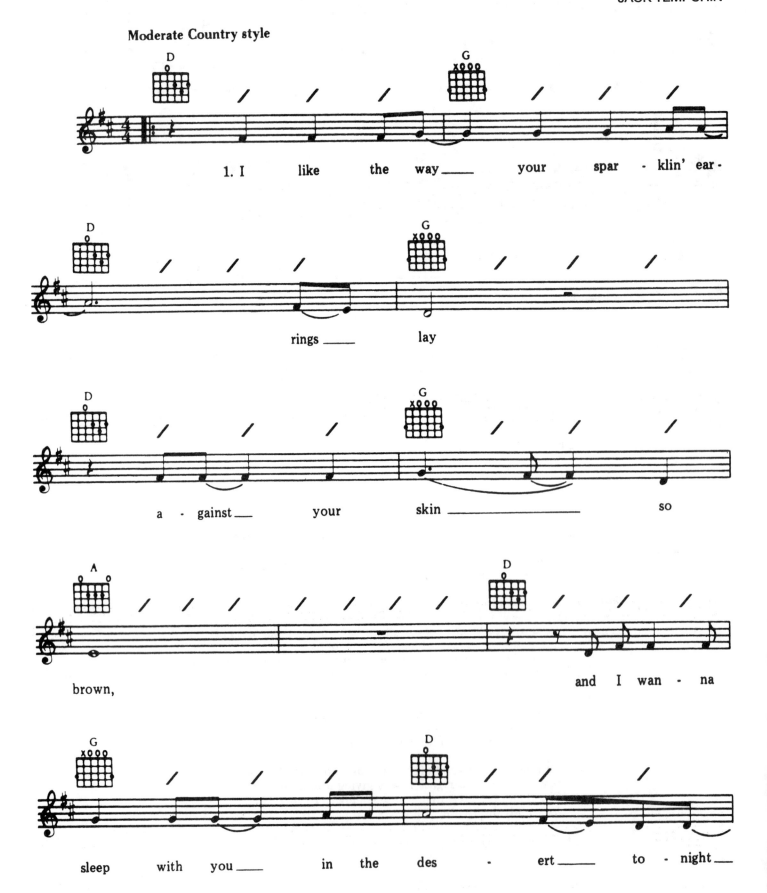

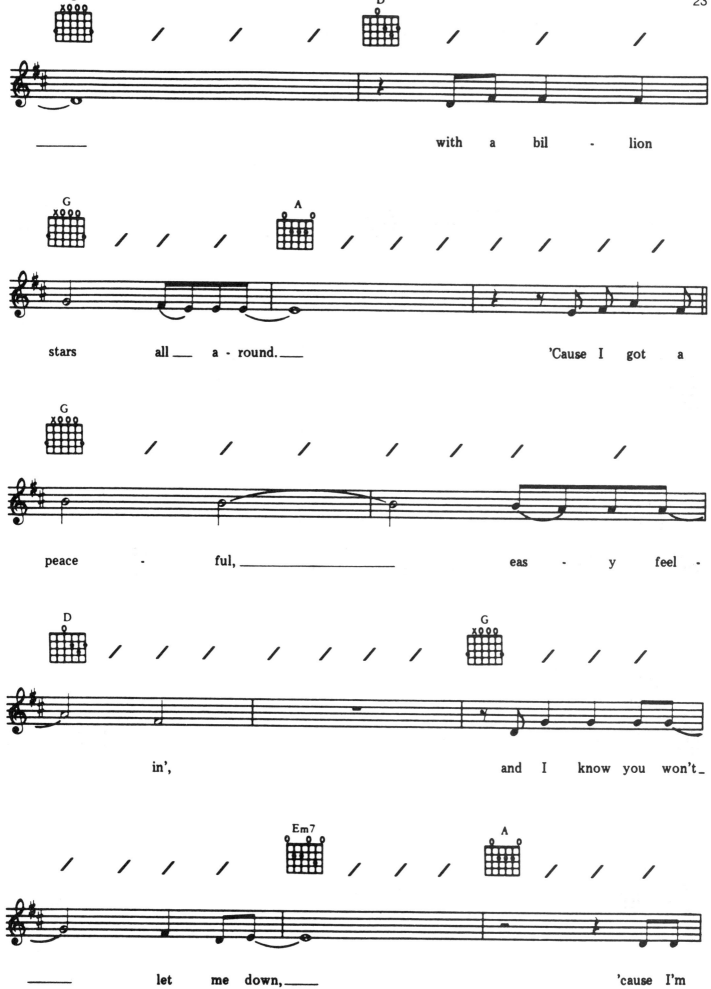

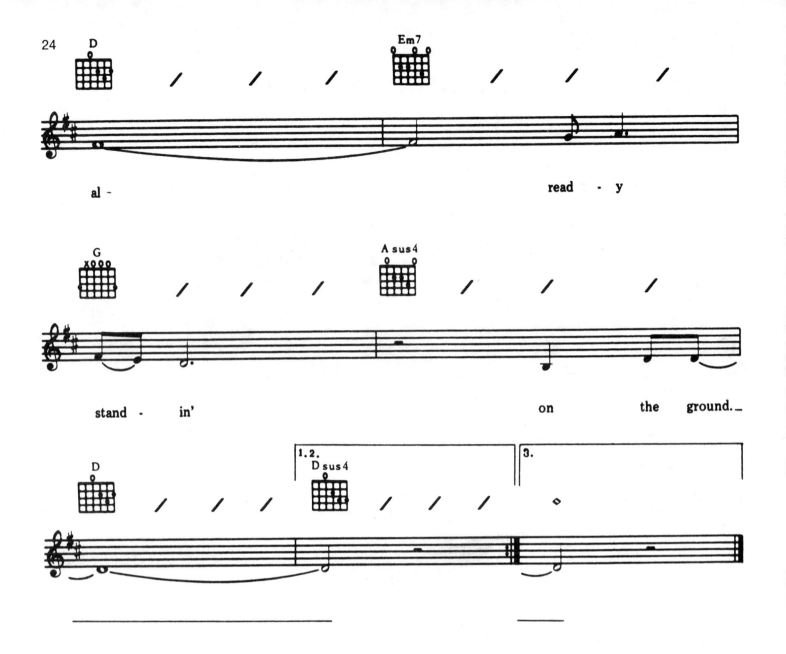

al -   read - y

stand - in'   on   the   ground.

2. And I found out a long time ago
   What a woman can do to your soul;
   Ah, but she can't take you anyway,
   You don't already know how to go.
   And I got a peaceful, easy feelin', (etc.)

3. I get the feelin' I may know you
   As a lover and a friend;
   But this voice keeps whisperin' in my other ear,
   Tells me I may never see you again.
   'Cause I got a peaceful, easy feelin', (etc.)

STAIRWAY TO HEAVEN

Words and Music by
JIMMY PAGE and ROBERT PLANT

A little faster, with a strong beat

TIN MAN

Words and Music by
DEWEY BUNNELL

say I'm spin - ning 'round, 'round, __ 'round, 'round; smoke glass_ stain __ bright col - or.

D. S. 𝄋 *(with repeats) al Coda* ✠

Im - age go - ing down, down, __ down, down; soap - suds_ green __ like bub - bles.

Coda

COBWEBS AND DUST

Words and Music by
GORDON LIGHTFOOT

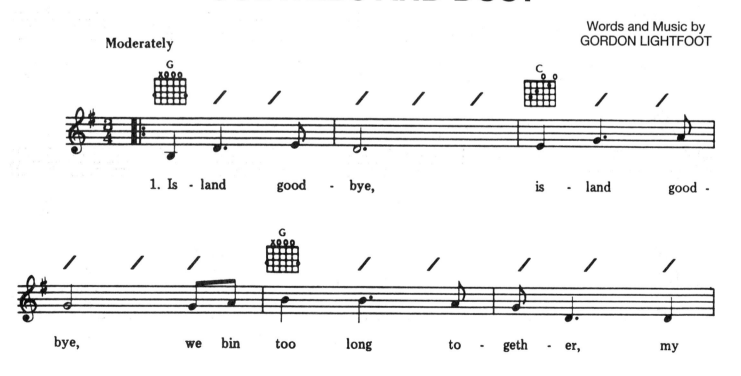

Moderately

1. Is - land good - bye, is - land good -

bye, we bin too long to - geth - er, my

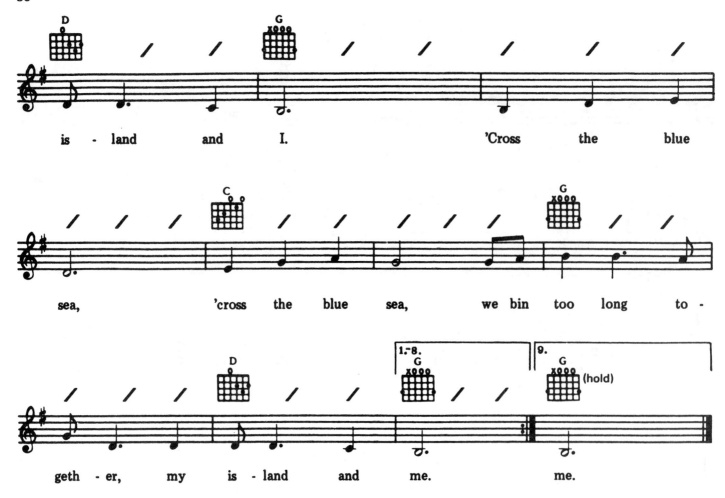

is - land and I.   'Cross the blue

sea,   'cross the blue sea,   we bin too long to -

geth - er,   my   is - land   and   me.   me.

Additional lyrics

2. Cobwebs and dust, cobwebs and dust,
   I hate to leave you but leave you I must.
   Float through the sky, float through the sky,
   We bin too long together, my cobwebs and I.

3. Unlock the gate, unlock the gate,
   Lower the drawbridge the hour is late.
   Whom shall it be, whom shall it be?
   We bin too long together, my drawbridge and me.

4. Troubles goodbye, troubles goodbye,
   We bin too long together, my troubles and I.
   'Cross the blue sea, 'cross the blue sea,
   We bin too long together, my troubles and me.

5. Cobwebs and dust, cobwebs and dust,
   I hate to leave you but leave you I must.
   Float through the sky, float through the sky,
   We bin too long together, my cobwebs and I.

6. Tear down the walls, tear down the walls,
   Gather my treasure and scatter it all.
   Whom shall it be, whom shall it be?
   We bin too long together, my treasure and me.

7. Kisses goodbye, kisses goodbye,
   We bin too long together, her kisses and I.
   'Cross the blue sea, 'cross the blue sea,
   We bin too long together, her kisses and me.

8. Cobwebs and dust, cobwebs and dust,
   I hate to leave you but leave you I must.
   Float through the sky, float through the sky,
   We bin too long together, my cobwebs and I.

9. Run to her side, run to her side,
   Run to my island and make her your bride.
   Whom shall it be, whom shall it be?
   We bin too long together, my island and me.

CINNAMON GIRL

Words and Music by
NEIL YOUNG

GIMME SOME LOVIN'

Words and Music by
STEVE WINWOOD, MUFF WINWOOD
and SPENCER DAVIS

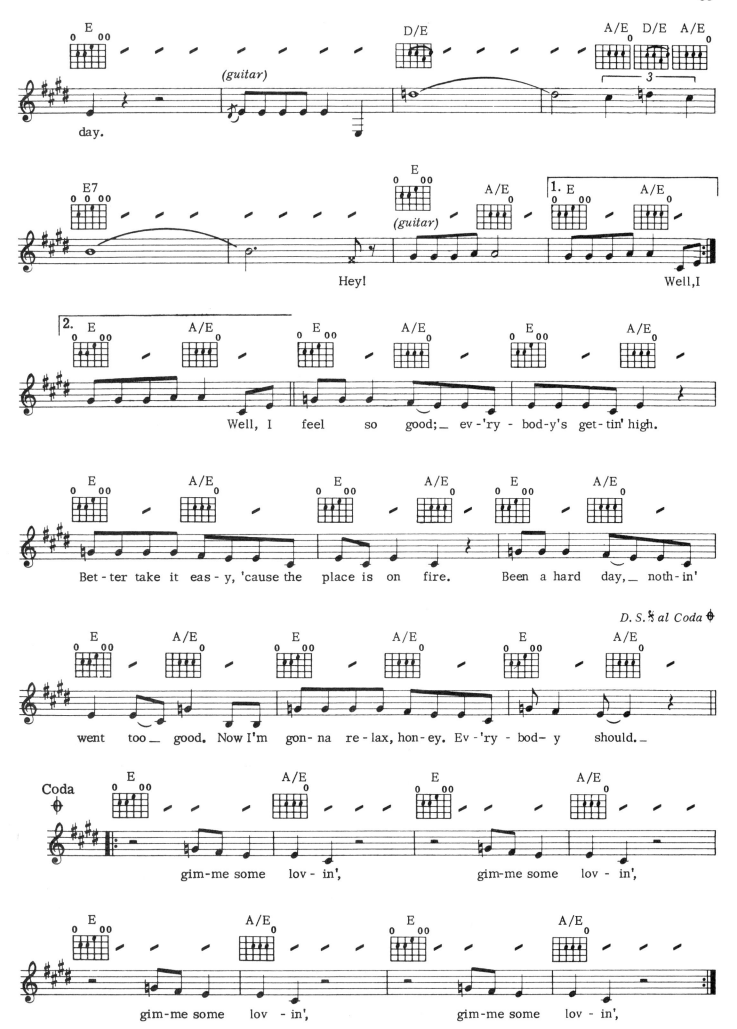

HEY HEY, MY MY (INTO THE BLACK)

Words and Music by
NEIL YOUNG

Medium Rock beat

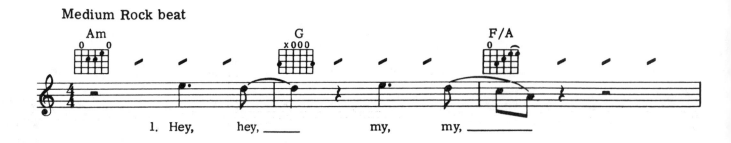

1. Hey, hey, _____ my, my, _____

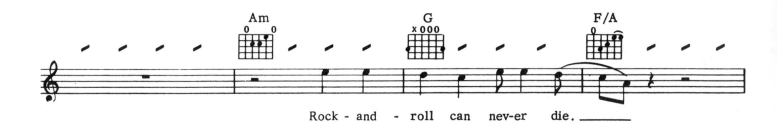

Rock - and - roll can nev-er die. _____

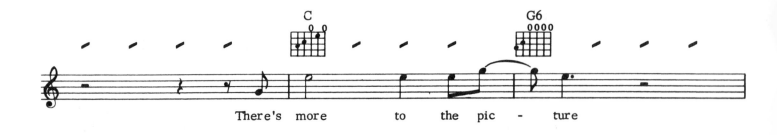

There's more to the pic - ture

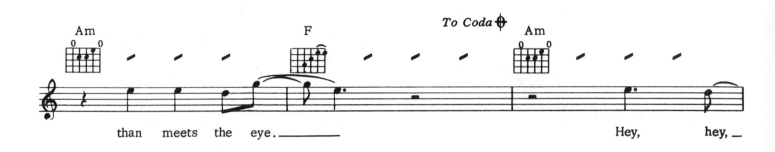

than meets the eye. _____ Hey, hey, _

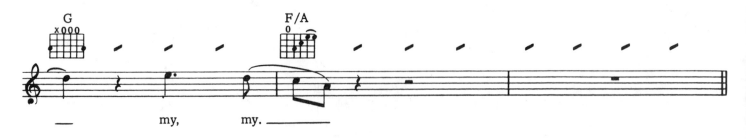

_ my, my. _____

(YOUR LOVE HAS LIFTED ME) HIGHER AND HIGHER

Words and Music by
GARY JACKSON,
CARL SMITH and RAYNARD MINER

THE SUMMER KNOWS
(Theme from " SUMMER of 42")

Lyric by
MARILYN and ALAN BERGMAN

Music by
MICHEL LEGRAND

MORE THAN I CAN SAY

Words and Music by
SONNY CURTIS and JERRY ALLISON

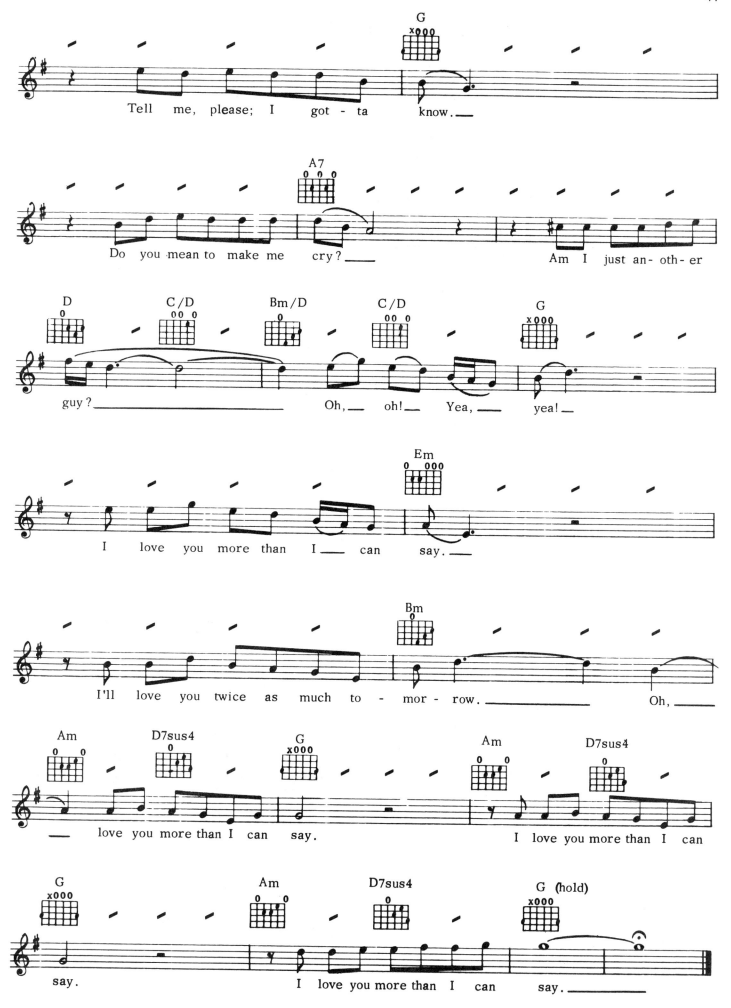

AFTER MIDNIGHT

Words and Music by
JOHN J. CALE

OLD MAN

Words and Music by
NEIL YOUNG

Slowly, in 2

Old man, look at my life; I'm a lot like you were.

Old man, look at my life; I'm a lot like

you were.

Old man, look at my life,
Lulla - bies look in your eyes,

twen - ty - four and there's so much more.
run a - round the same old town,

Live a - lone in a
does - n't mean that

par - a - dise___ that makes me think___ of two._____ Love lost,
much to me___ to mean that much___ to you._____ I've been

such a cost,___ give me things that don't get lost
first and last; ___ look at how the time goes past.

/

I CAN'T TELL YOU WHY

Words and Music by
DON HENLEY,
GLENN FREY and TIMOTHY B. SCHMIT

SAIL AWAY

Words and Music by
RANDY NEWMAN

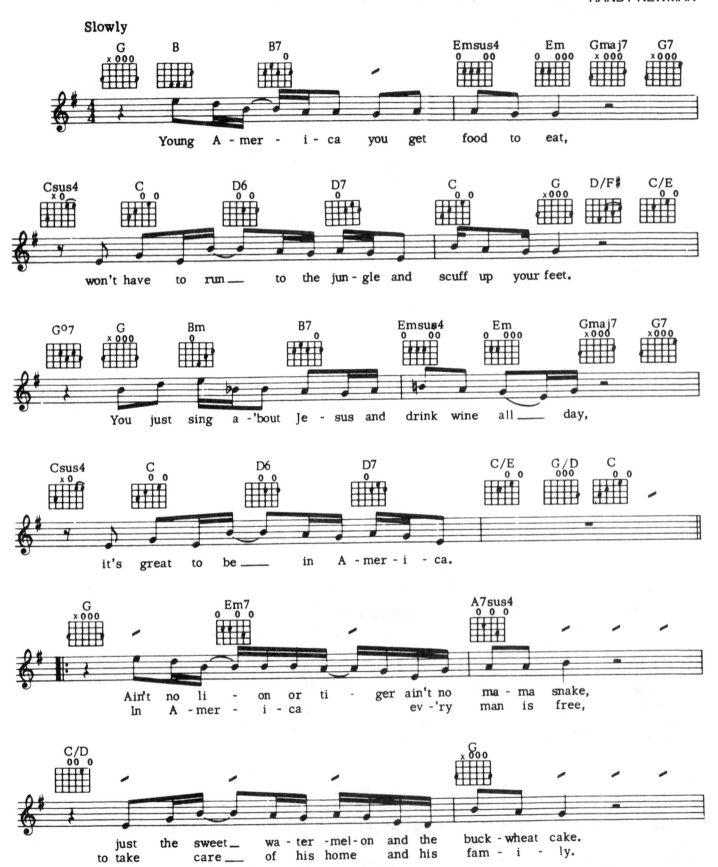

FIRE LAKE

Words and Music by
BOB SEGER & THE SILVER BULLET BAND

Bridge

Who wants to brave those bronze beau - ties, ly - in' in the sun with their long, soft hair fall - in', fly-in' as they run? Oh, they smile so shy and they flirt so well __ and they lay you down __ so fast __ till you look straight up __ and say, "Oh Lord, am I real-ly here at last?"

And head out. __

Repeat and fade

__ Who wants to go to Fire Lake? __

And head out. __

Additional lyrics

2. Who wants to break the news about Uncle Joe?
   You remember Uncle Joe. He was the one afraid to cut the cake.
   Who wants to tell poor Aunt Sarah
   Joe's run off to Fire Lake?
   Joe's run off to Fire Lake?

   Bridge

3. Who wants to play those eights and aces?
   Who wants a raise? Who needs a stake?
   Who wants to take that long-shot gamble
   And head out to Fire Lake?

LOVE IS ALL AROUND

Words and Music by
SONNY CURTIS

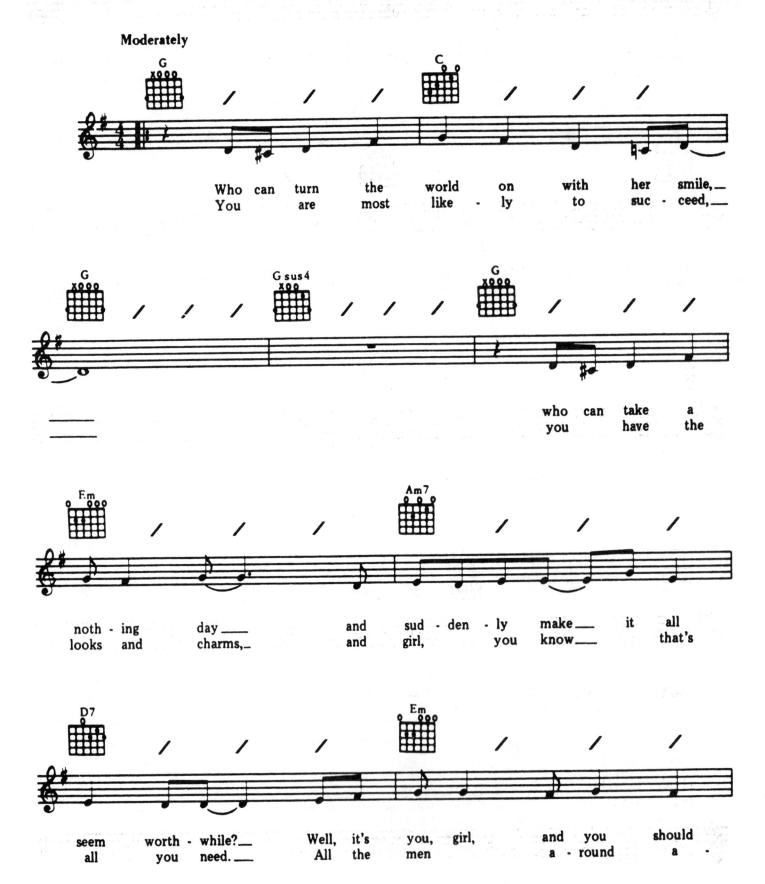

53

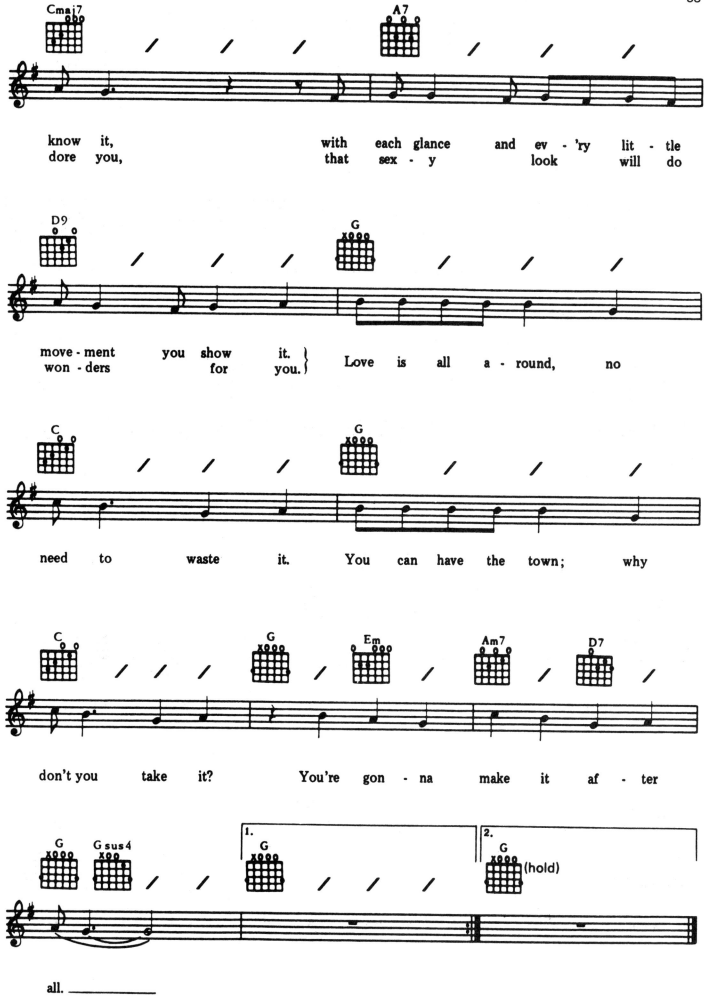

know it, with each glance and ev-'ry lit-tle
dore you, that sex-y look will do

move-ment you show it. } Love is all a-round, no
won-ders you show for you. }

need to waste it. You can have the town; why

don't you take it? You're gon-na make it af-ter

all. _____

THE WRECK OF THE EDMUND FITZGERALD

Words and Music by
GORDON LIGHTFOOT

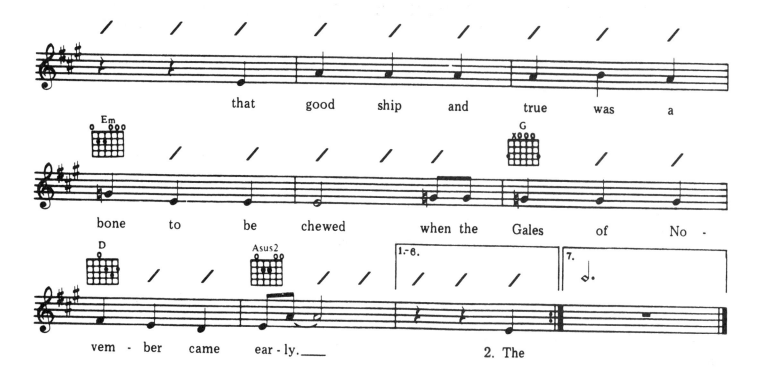

that good ship and true was a

bone to be chewed when the Gales of No -

vem - ber came ear - ly.___ 2. The

2. The ship was the pride of the American side coming back from some mill in Wisconsin.
As the big freighters go it was bigger than most with a crew and good captain well seasoned,
Concluding some terms with a couple of steel firms when they left fully loaded for Cleveland.
And later that night when the ship's bell rang, could it be the north wind they'd been feelin'?

3. The wind in the wires made a tattletale sound and a wave broke over the railing.
And every man knew as the captain did too 'twas the witch of November come stealin'.
The dawn came late and the breakfast had to wait when the Gales of November came slashin'.
When afternoon came it was freezin' rain in the face of a hurricane west wind.

4. When suppertime came the old cook came on deck sayin', "Fellas, it's too rough t' feed ya."
At seven P.M. a main hatchway caved in; he said, "Fellas, it's bin good t' know ya'."
The captain wired in he had water comin' in and the good ship and crew was in peril.
And later that night when 'is lights went outta sight came the wreck of the Edmund Fitzgerald.

5. Does anyone know where the love of God goes when the waves turn the minutes to hours.
The searchers all say they'd have made Whitefish Bay if they'd put fifteen more miles behind 'er.
They might have split up or they might have capsized; they may have broke deep and took water.
And all that remains is the faces and the names of the wives and the sons and the daughters.

6. Lake Huron rolls, Superior swings in the rooms of her ice-water mansion.
Old Michigan steams like a young man's dreams; the islands and bays are for sportsmen.
And farther below Lake Ontario takes in what Lake Erie can send her,
And the iron boats go as the mariners all know with the Gales of November remembered.

7. In a musty old hall in Detroit they prayed, in the "Maritime Sailors' Cathedral."
The church bell chimed 'til it rang twenty-nine times for each man on the Edmund Fitzgerald.
The legend lives on from the Chippewa on down of the big lake they called "Gitche Gumee."
"Superior," they said, "never gives up her dead when the Gales of November come early!"

LE FREAK

Words and Music by
BERNARD EDWARDS and NILE RODGERS

LONELY PEOPLE

Words and Music by
DAN PEEK and CATHERINE L. PEEK

Moderately fast

JULIA DREAM

Words and Music by
ROGER WATERS

dreams. ___

dreams. ___

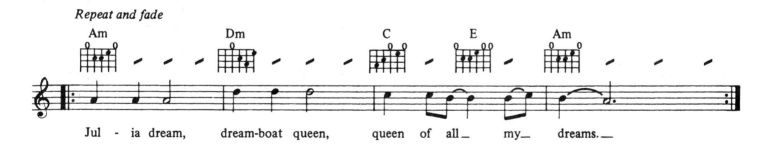

Jul - ia dream,   dream-boat queen,   queen of all ___ my ___ dreams. ___

WORKIN' AT THE CAR WASH BLUES

Words and Music by
JIM CROCE

air con-di-tioned of-fice in a swiv-el chair,

talk-in' some trash to the sec-re-tar-ies, say-in', *"Here, now, mam-ma, come on o-ver*

here." In-stead, I'm stuck here rub-bin' these fen-ders with a rag___ and

walk-in' home in sog-gy old shoes with them stead-i-ly de-press-in',

low down___ mind-mess-in' work-in' at the car-wash blues.___ You know a

man of my a-bil-i-ty,___ he should be smok-in' on a big___ ci-

gar. But till I get my-self straight___ I guess I'll just have to wait___ in my

BOULEVARD

Medium Rock beat

Words and Music by
JACKSON BROWNE

Down on the Boul - e - vard _ they take it _ hard. _____
kid's in shock _ up and down the _ block. _____

They look at life _ with such dis - re - gard. _
The folks are home _ play - ing Beat the Clock. _

They say it can't be won _____ the way the
Down at the Gold - en Cup _____ they set the

game is run. _____ But if you choose to stay, _
young ones up _____ un - der the ne - on light, _

you wind up play - ing an - y way. It's o - kay. _____
sell - ing day for night.

The It's al - right.

66

LOVE IN THE FIRST DEGREE

Words and music by
JIM HURT and TIM DuBOISE

69

LONESOME LOSER

Words and Music by
DAVID BRIGGS

Moderately

Tacet

Have you   heard a - bout the lone - some   los - er,   beat - en

by the Queen of Hearts ev - 'ry time?   Have you   heard a - bout the lone - some

los - er?   He's a   los - er, but he still keeps on   try - ing.

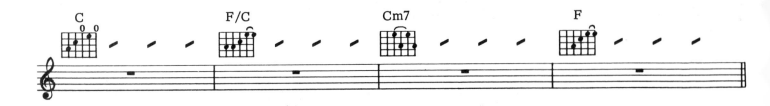

C   F/C   Cm7   F

C   F/C   Cm7

Sit down.__   Take a look at your - self.__   Don't you want__ to
Un - luck - y in love, least that's   what   they say.__   He lost his head and he

F/C   C   F/C

be some - bod - y?   Some - day, some - bod - y's gon - na   see in - side.   You
gam - bled his heart a - way.   He still keeps search - in', though there's noth - in' left.   He

ANGIE BABY

Words and Music by
ALAN O'DAY

Moderately slow

You live your life in the songs you hear on the
Lovers ap - pear in your room each night and they
head - lines read that a boy disappeared, and

rock-and-roll ra - di - o, _____ and when a young girl does-n't
whirl you 'cross the floor, _____ but they al - ways seem to
ev - 'ry-one thinks he died ___ 'cept a cra - zy girl with a

have an - y friends that's a real - ly nice place to go. _____
fade a - way when your dad - dy taps on your door. _____
se - cret lov - er who keeps her sat - is - fied. _____

Folks hop - in' you'd turn out cool, but they had to take you
Angie girl, are you all right? Tell the ra - di -
It's so nice to be in - sane; no one asks you

out of school. You're a lit - tle touched, you know, An - gie
o good - night. All a - lone once more, An - gie
to ex - plain. Ra - di - o by your side, An - gie

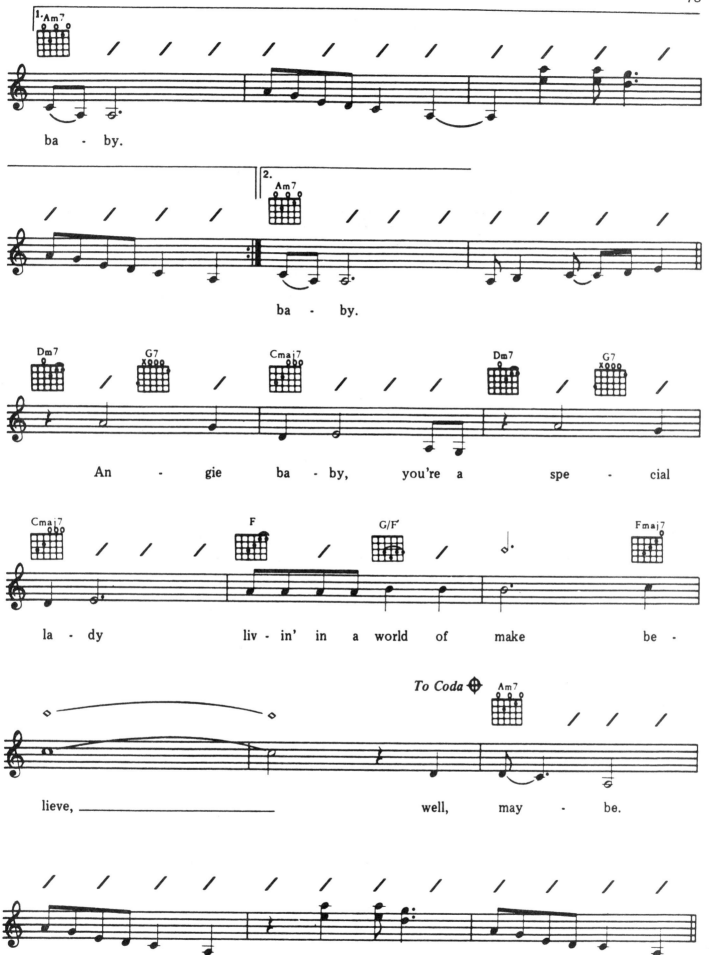

ba - by.

ba - by.

An - gie ba - by, you're a spe - cial

la - dy liv - in' in a world of make be -

To Coda

lieve, _____ well, may - be.

74

IF YOU COULD READ MY MIND

Words and Music by
GORDON LIGHTFOOT

ghost that you can't see.
just too hard to take.

I'd walk a - way___ like a mov - ie star who gets burned in a three way

script. En - ter num - ber two: a mov-ie queen to

play the scene of bring - ing all the good things out of me. But for

now, love, let's be real; I nev-er thought I could

act this way, and I've got to say that I just don't get it.

I don't know where we went wrong, but the feel-ing's gone and I

D. C. (Lyric 1) al Coda ⊕

THE BEST OF MY LOVE

Words and Music by
DON HENLEY,
GLENN FREY and JOHN DAVID SOUTHER

LOVE IS A ROSE

Words and Music by
NEIL YOUNG

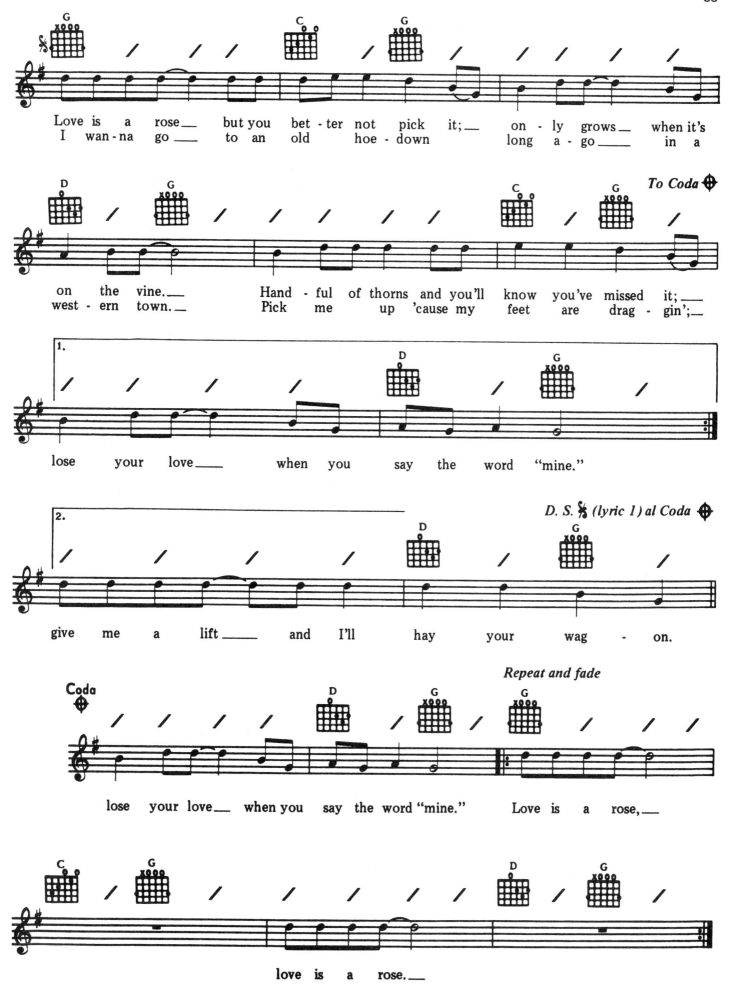

BARBARA ANN

Words and Music by
FRED FASSERT

85

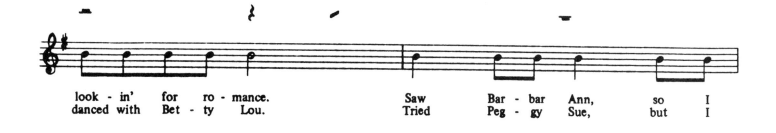

look - in' for ro - mance. Saw Bar - bar Ann, so I
danced with Bet - ty Lou. Tried Peg - gy Sue, but I

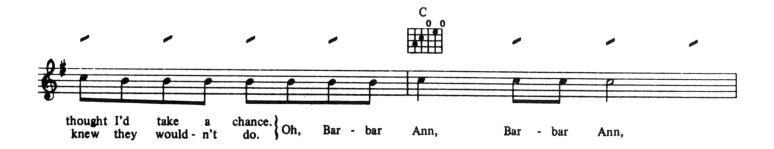

thought I'd take a chance. } Oh, Bar - bar Ann, Bar - bar Ann,
knew they would - n't do.

take my hand. Oh, Bar - bar Ann, Bar - bar Ann, take my hand. You got me

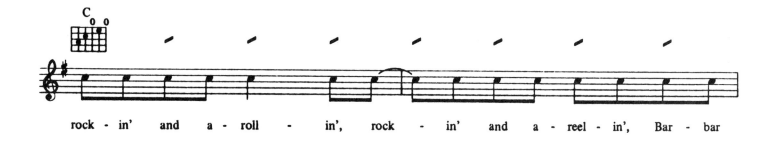

rock - in' and a - roll - in', rock - in' and a - reel - in', Bar - bar

1.　　　　　　　　2.　　　　D.C. al Fine

Ann, Bar - bar - bar - bar - bar Ann.　　　bar - bar Ann.

LYIN' EYES

Words and Music by
DON HENLEY and GLENN FREY

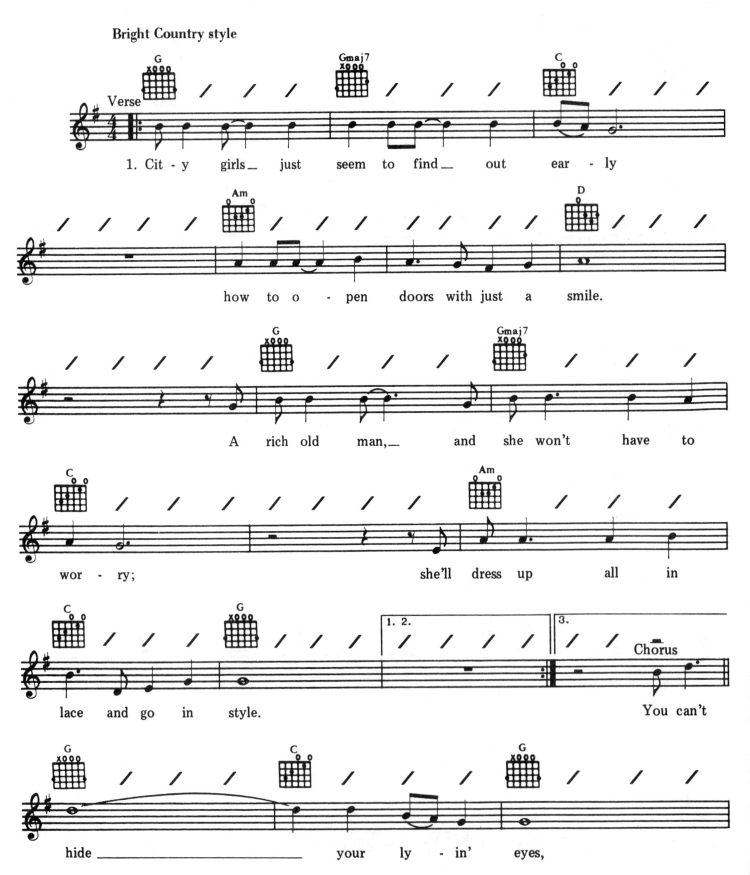

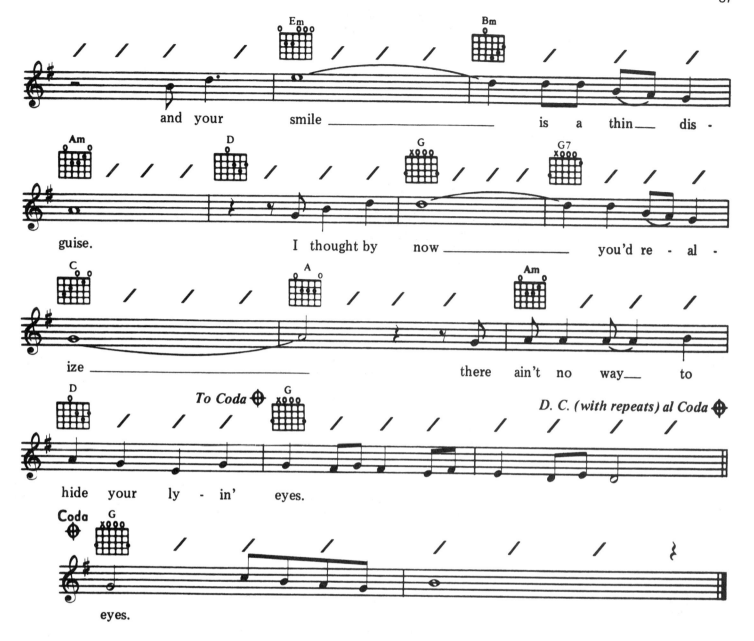

and your smile _____ is a thin ___ dis-

guise. I thought by now _____ you'd re - al -

ize _____ there ain't no way ___ to

To Coda ⊕   *D. C. (with repeats) al Coda* ⊕

hide your ly - in' eyes.

Coda ⊕

eyes.

2. Late at night a big old house gets lonely;
   I guess every form of refuge has its price.
   And it breaks her heart to think her love is only
   Given to a man with hands as cold as ice.

3. So she tells him she must go out for the evening
   To comfort an old friend who's feelin' down.
   But he knows where she's goin' as she's leavin';
   She is headed for the cheatin' side of town.
   (Chorus)

4. She gets up and pours herself a strong one
   And stares out at the stars up in the sky.
   Another night, it's gonna be a long one;
   She draws the shade and hangs her head to cry.

5. My, oh my, you sure know how to arrange things;
   You set it up so well, so carefully.
   Ain't it funny how your new life didn't change things;
   You're still the same old girl you used to be.
   (Chorus)

DAISY JANE

Words and Music by
GERRY BECKLEY

play-in' my cra-zy game, game.
guess you're real-ly to blame, blame.

Does she real-ly love me? I think ___ she does. ___
Do you real-ly love me? I hope ___ you do. ___

— Like the stars a - bove me, I know ___ be - cause ___
— Like the stars a - bove me, how I _____ love you _____

— when the sky is bright, ___ ev - 'ry - thing's ___ all ___
— when it's cold at night, ___ ev - 'ry - thing's ___ all ___

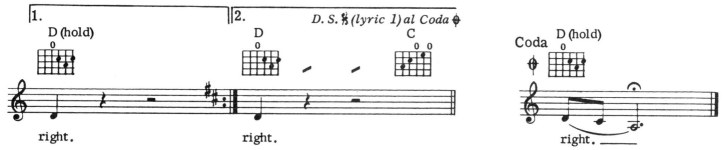

right.   right.   right. ___

HEARTACHE TONIGHT

Words and Music by
DON HENLEY, GLENN FREY,
BOB SEGER and JOHN DAVID SOUTHER

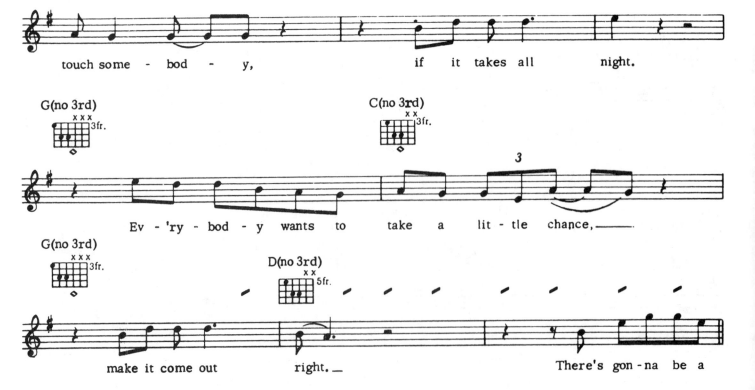

heart - ache to-night,   a heart - ache to-night I know. ____

To Coda

There's gon-na be a heart - ache to-night,   a heart - ache to-night I know. _

____   Lord, I   know. _   Some peo-ple like to

stay out late. _   Some folks can't hold out that long. _   But

no - bod - y wants to go home now; _   there's too much go-in' on.

This night is gon-na last for - ev - er.

Last all, last all sum-mer long.   Some time be-fore the

sun comes up ____   the ra - di - o is gon - na play that song. _

There's gon-na be a heart-ache to-night, a heart-ache to-night, I know.—

There's gon-na be a heart-ache to-night, a

heart-ache to-night, I know. Lord, I know.— There's gon-na be a

heart-ache to-night, the moon's shin-in' bright, so turn out the light, and

we'll get it right.— There's gon-na be a heart-ache to-night,— a

heart-ache to-night, I know.—

D.S. al Coda

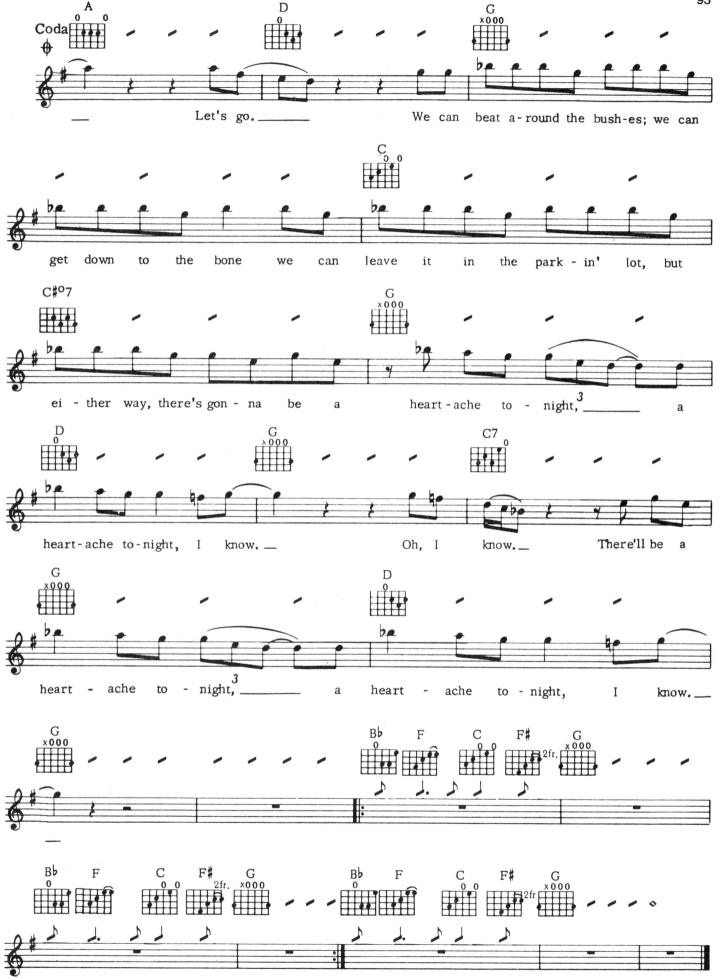

COOL CHANGE

Words and Music by
GLENN SHORROCK

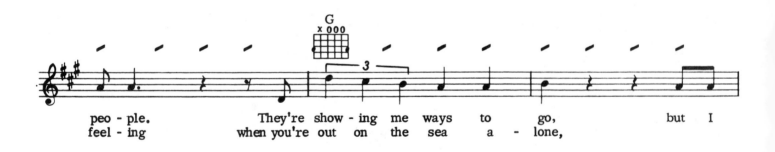

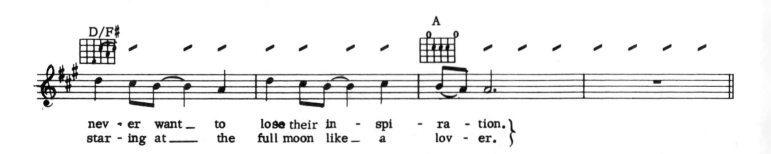

let me breathe_ the air._____

If there's one thing in my life _ that's miss - ing, it's the

time that I spend a - lone, sail - ing on the

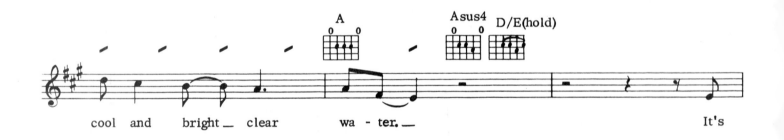

cool and bright_ clear wa - ter._ It's

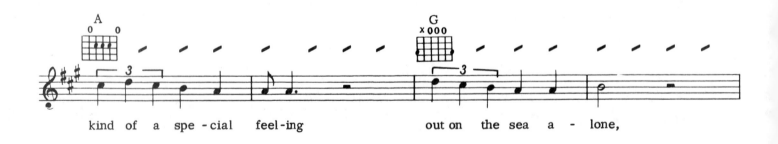

kind of a spe - cial feel - ing out on the sea a - lone,

star - ing at the full moon like a lov - er._____

THIS IS IT

Words and Music by
KENNY LOGGINS and MICHAEL McDONALD

YOU'RE SIXTEEN

Words and Music by
BOB SHERMAN and DICK SHERMAN

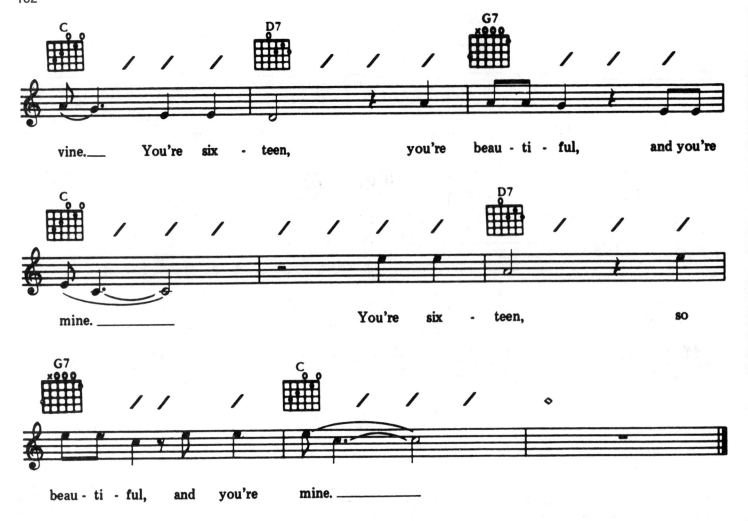

vine.___ You're six - teen, you're beau - ti - ful, and you're

mine. _____ You're six - teen, so

beau - ti - ful, and you're mine. _____

WHOLE LOTTA LOVE

Words and Music by
JIMMY PAGE, ROBERT PLANT
JOHN PAUL JONES and JOHN BONHAM

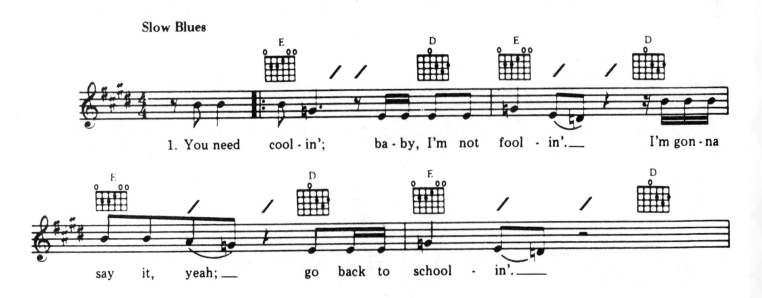

Slow Blues

1. You need cool - in'; ba - by, I'm not fool - in'.___ I'm gon - na

say it, yeah; ___ go back to school - in'. ___

Way down in - side, ___ hon - ey, you need it.

I'm gon-na give you my love, ___ I'm gon - na give you my love. ___

Wan - na whole lot - ta love? Wan - na whole lot - ta

love? Wan - na whole lot - ta love? Wan - na whole lot - ta

1.2.   love.   2. You've been   3.   love.

Repeat and fade

2. You've been learnin', baby, I mean learnin'.
   All them good times, baby, I've been yearnin'.
   Way down inside, (etc.)

3. You've been coolin'; baby, I've been droolin'.
   All the good times I've been misusin'.
   Way down inside, (etc.)

HE AIN'T HEAVY . . . HE'S MY BROTHER

Words by
BOB RUSSELL

Music by
BOBBY SCOTT

lad - en   at all,_____   I'm lad - en   with

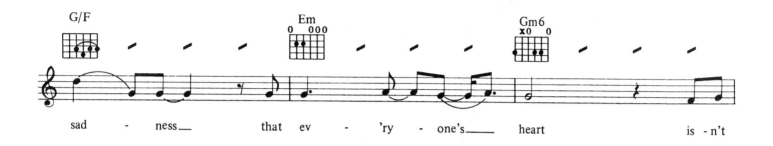

sad - ness___   that ev - 'ry - one's___ heart   is - n't

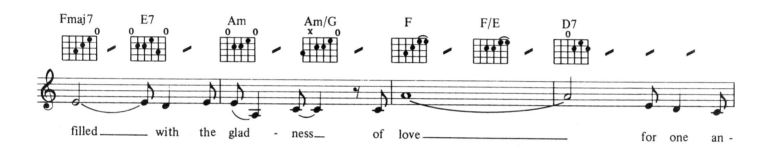

filled_____ with   the glad - ness___   of love _____   for one   an -

D.S. al Coda

Coda

oth - er.___   Verse Tacet   It's a   long,   long

2. So on we go. His welfare is my concern.
No burden is he to bear. We'll get there,
For I know he would not encumber me.
He ain't heavy, he's my brother.

Bridge

3. It's a long, long road from which there is no return.
While we're on our way to there, why not share?
And the load doesn't weigh me down at all.
He ain't heavy, he's my brother.

MINUTE BY MINUTE

Words by
MICHAEL McDONALD and LESTER ABRAMS

Music by
MICHAEL McDONALD

LET'S HANG ON

Words and Music by
BOB CREWE,
SANDY LINZER and DENNY RANDELL

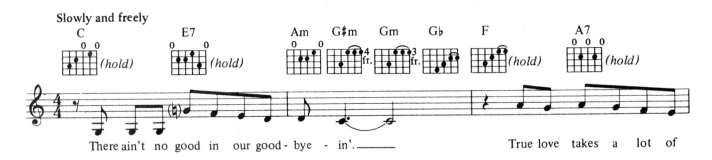

There ain't no good in our good-bye - in'. ____ True love takes a lot of

try - in'. Oh, ____ I'm cry - in'. Let's hang on ____

____ to what we've got. ____ Don't let go, ____ girl; we've got a

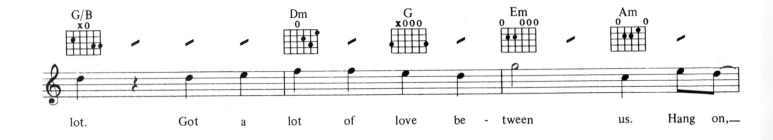

lot. Got a lot of love be - tween us. Hang on, ____

____ hang on, ____ hang on ____ to what we've got. ____

1. You say you're gon - na go and call it quits,— gon - na

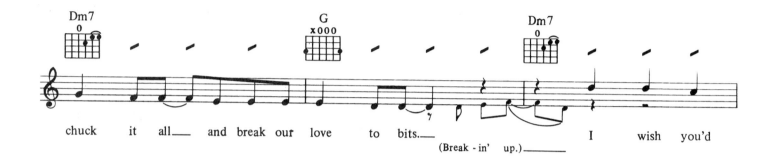

chuck it all— and break our love to bits.— I wish you'd
(Break - in' up.)———

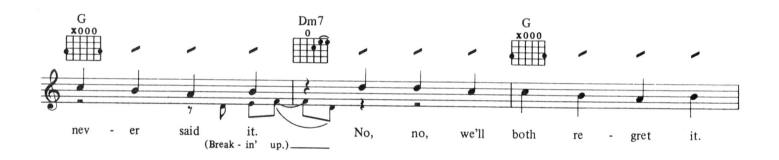

nev - er said it. No, no, we'll both re - gret it.
(Break - in' up.)———

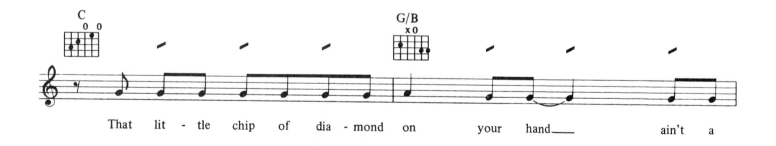

That lit - tle chip of dia - mond on your hand— ain't a

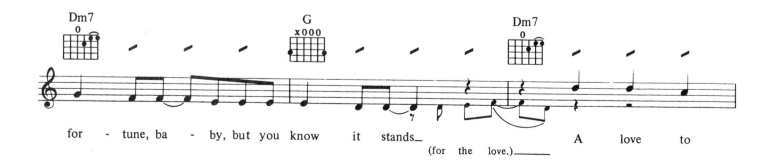

for - tune, ba - by, but you know it stands— A love to
(for the love.)———

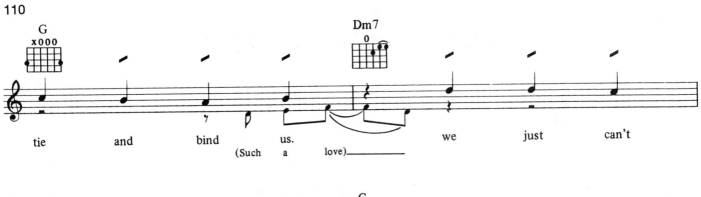

tie and bind us. (Such a love)_____ we just can't

leave be - hind us. Ba - by,_____ (Don't you go.)_____

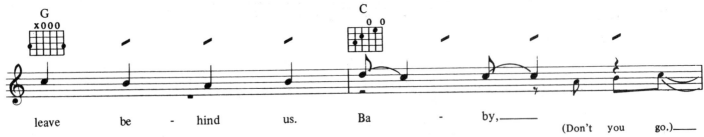

ba - by,_____ (No, no, no.)_____ ba - by, (Think it o - ver and

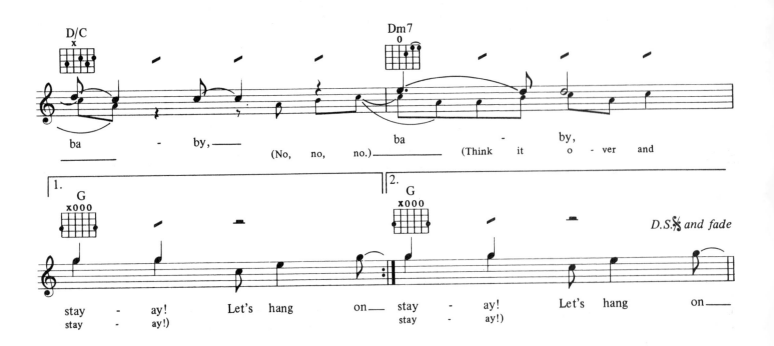

stay - ay! Let's hang on___ stay - ay! Let's hang on_____
stay - ay!) stay - ay!)

D.S.𝄋 and fade

2. There isn't anything I wouldn't do.
   I'd pay any price to get in good with you.
   (Patch it up.) Give me a second turnin'.
   (Patch it up.) Don't cool off while I'm burnin'.
   You've got me cryin', dyin' at your door.
   Don't shut me out, ooh, let me in once more.
   (Open up) your arms; I need to hold you.
   (Open up) your heart; oh girl, I told you.
   Baby, (Don't you go.)
   Baby, (No, no, no.)
   Baby, (Think it over and stay - ay!)

Good Girls Don't

Words and Music by
DOUG FIEGER

Chorus

"Good girls don't, ____ good girls don't."_

_ But she'll be tell-in' you, "Good girls don't, _____ but I_

_ do." 2. So you And it's a

teen-age _ sad-ness ev-'ry one has got to taste, _

_ an in-be-tween age_ mad-ness that you

To Coda ⊕

know you. can't_e-rase____ till she's sit-tin' on_ your face. _

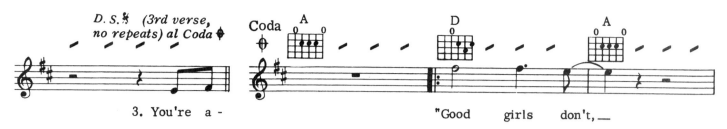

D. S. 𝄋 (3rd verse, no repeats) al Coda ✛

Coda

3. You're a -

"Good   girls   don't, __

good   girls   don't."__ But she'll be tell-in' you, "Good   girls

1.

don't, _____ but I _____ do."

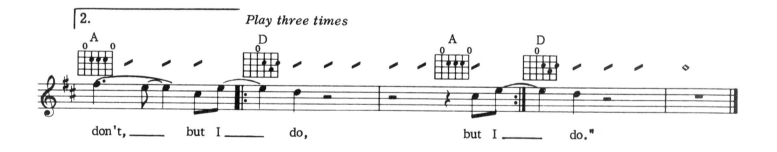

2.   *Play three times*

don't, _____ but I _____ do,   but I _____ do."

Additional lyrics

2. So you call her on the phone
   To talk about the teachers that you hate.
   And she says she's all alone,
   And her parents won't be coming home til late.
   There's a ringing in your brain,
   'Cause you could have swore you thought you heard her saying;

   Chorus

3. You're alone with her at last,
   And you're waiting till you think the time is right.
   'Cause you've heard she's pretty fast,
   And you're hoping that she'll give you some tonight:
   So you start to make your play,
   'Cause you could have swore you thought you heard her saying;

   Chorus

TIME IN A BOTTLE

Words and Music by
JIM CROCE

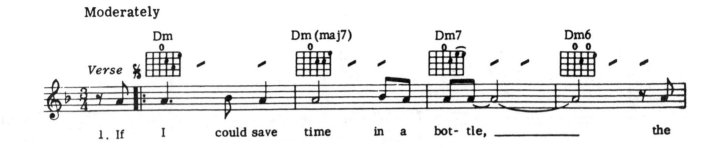

Verse

1. If I could save time in a bot- tle, _____ the

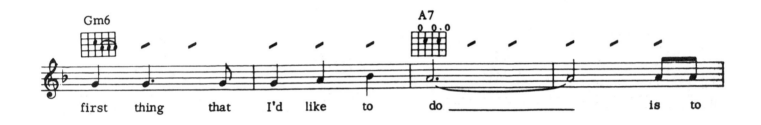

first thing that I'd like to do _____ is to

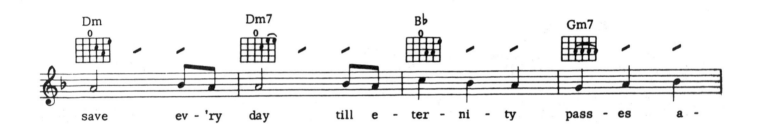

save ev- 'ry day till e - ter - ni - ty pass - es a -

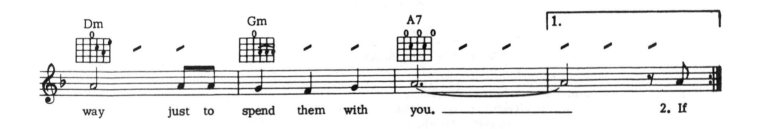

way just to spend them with you. _____

2. If

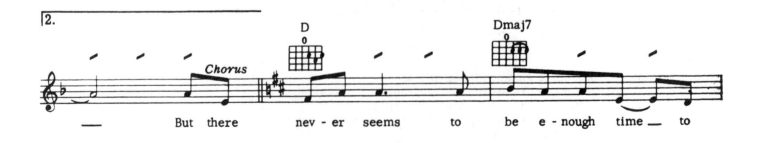

Chorus

___ But there nev - er seems to be e - nough time ___ to

do the things you want to do once you find them. _____

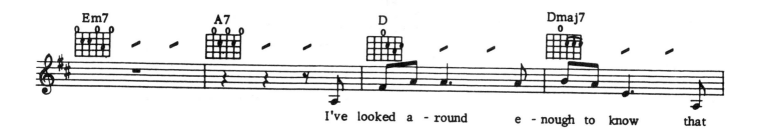

I've looked a - round e - nough to know that

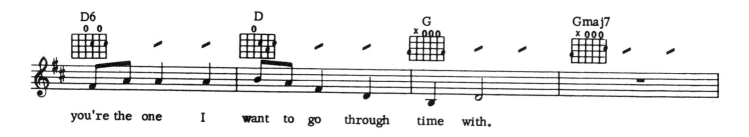

you're the one I want to go through time with.

3. If

Additional lyrics

2. If I could make days last forever,
   If words could make wishes come true,
   I'd save every day like a treasure, and then
   Again I would spend them with you.

   (Chorus)

3. If I had a box just for wishes,
   And dreams that had never come true,
   The box would be empty except for the memory of
   How they were answered by you.

   (Chorus)

MY BEST FRIEND'S GIRL

Words and Music by
RIC OCASEK

She's my best friend's girl,   she's my best friend's

girl, _____ and she used to be mine. ___

To Coda ⊕

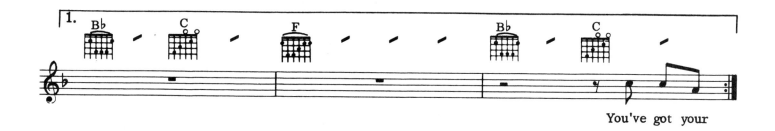

1.

You've got your

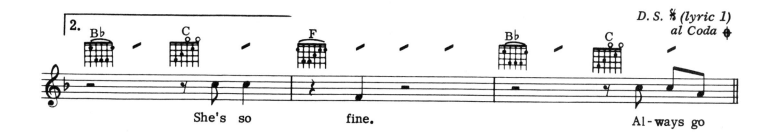

2.

D.S. % *(lyric 1)*
al Coda ⊕

She's so fine.   Al-ways go

Coda ⊕

She's so fine.

Repeat and fade

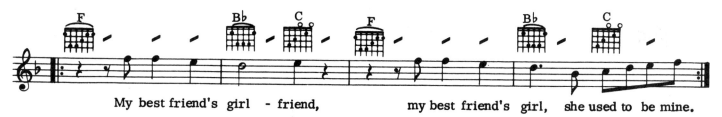

My best friend's girl - friend,   my best friend's girl, she used to be mine.

WHAT A FOOL BELIEVES

Words and Music by
MICHAEL McDONALD
and KENNY LOGGINS

Medium Rock beat

119

AFTER THE GOLD RUSH

Words and Music by
NEIL YOUNG

Look at Moth-er Na - ture on the run__ in the nine-teen sev-en - ties. Look at Moth-er Na - ture on the run__ in the nine-teen sev-en - ties. 2. I was lie. 3. Well, I new home.____

2. I was lyin' in a burned-out basement with the full moon in my eyes.
I was hopin' for replacement when the sun burst through the sky.
There was a band playin' in my head and I felt like getting high.
I was thinkin' about what a friend had said, I was hopin' it was a lie.
Thinkin' about what a friend had said, I was hopin' it was a lie.

3. Well, I dreamed I saw the silver spaceships flyin' in the yellow haze of the sun.
There were children cryin' and colors flyin' all around the chosen ones.
All in a dream, all in a dream, the loading had begun.
Flying Mother Nature's silver seed to a new home in the sun.
Flying Mother Nature's silver seed to a new home.

HELLO STRANGER

Words and Music by
BARBARA LEWIS

Bridge

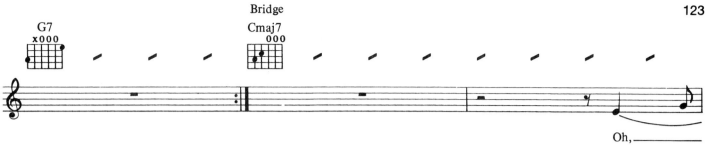

Oh,

yes, I'm so glad

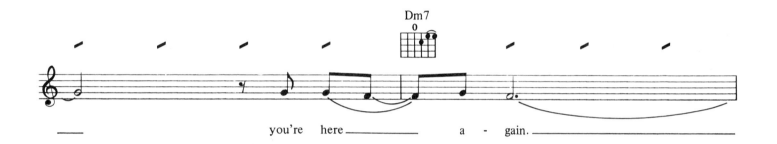

you're here a - gain.

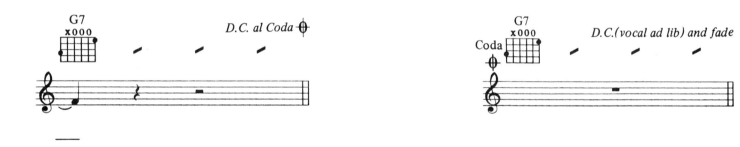

D.C. al Coda ⊕

Coda ⊕ *D.C.(vocal ad lib) and fade*

2. Oh, my, my, my, my, I'm so glad
   You stopped by to say hello to me.
   Remember that's the way it used to be?
   Ooh, it seems like a mighty long time.
   Shoo-bop shoo-bop, my baby.
   Ooh, it seems like a mighty long time.

   Bridge

3. Oh, if you're not gonna stay,
   Please don't tease me like you did before,
   Because I still love you so,
   Although it seems like a mighty long time.
   Shoo-bop shoo-bop, my baby.
   Ooh it seems like a mighty long time.

124

REMINISCING

Words and Music by
GRAHAM GOBLE

125

CRIMSON AND CLOVER

Words and music by
TOMMY JAMES and PETER LUCIA

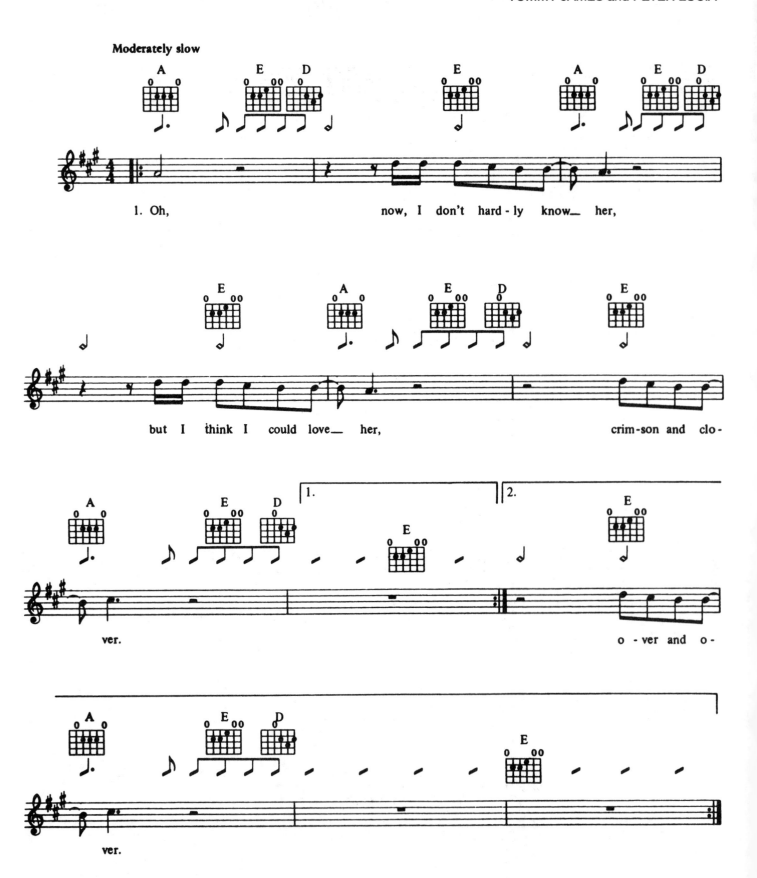

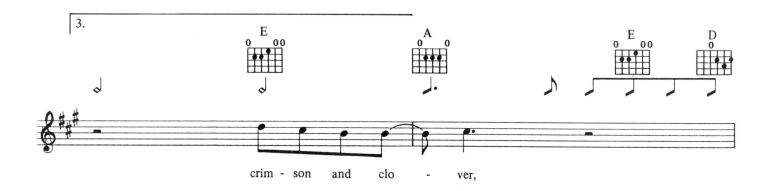

crim - son and clo - ver,

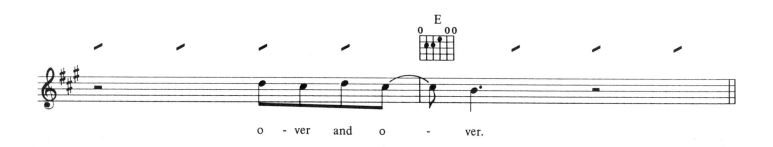

o - ver and o - ver.

Repeat and fade

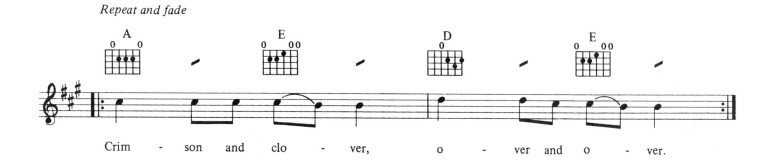

Crim - son and clo - ver, o - ver and o - ver.

2. Oh, I wish she'd come walking over.
   Now I been waiting to show her,
   Crimson and clover,
   Over and over.

3. Yes, my, my, such a sweet thing.
   I want to do everything.
   What a beautiful feeling,
   Crimson and clover,
   Over and over.

THE HUSTLE

By
VAN McCOY

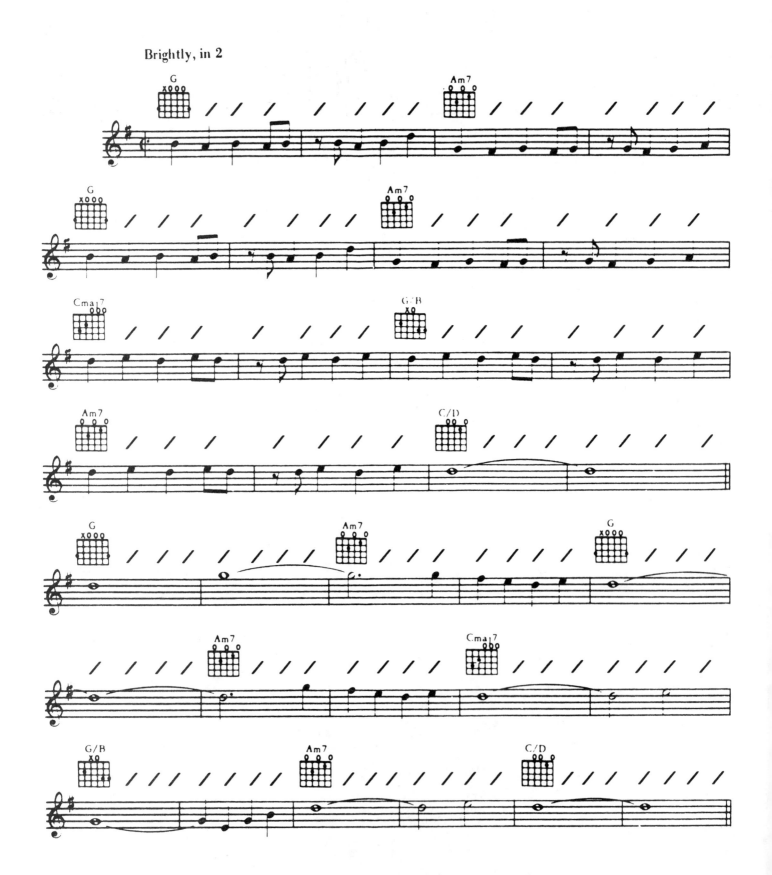

Do the Hus - tle!

Tacet

D. C. and fade

SANDMAN

Words and Music by
DEWEY BUNNELL

AS TEARS GO BY

Words and Music by
MICK JAGGER, KEITH RICHARDS
and **ANDREW LOOG OLDHAM**

2. My riches can't buy everything.
   I want to hear the children sing.
   All I hear is the sound of rain
     falling on the ground.
   I sit and watch as tears go by.

3. It is the evening of the day.
   I sit and watch the children play,
   Doing things I used to do
     they think are new.
   I sit and watch as tears go by.

SISTER GOLDEN HAIR

Words and Music by
GERRY BECKLEY

133

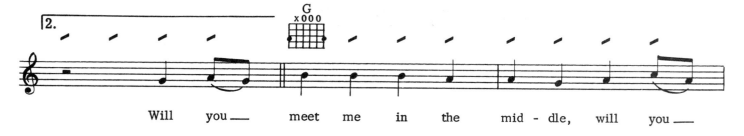

Will you ___ meet me in the mid - dle, will you ___

meet me in the air? _____ Will you love me just a

lit - tle, just e - nough to show you care? _____ Though I

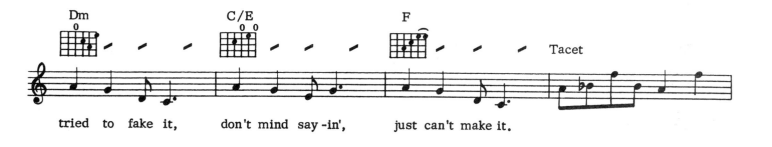

tried to fake it, don't mind say -in', just can't make it.

Mac ARTHUR PARK

Words and Music by
JIMMY WEBB

CHELSEA MORNING

Words and Music by
JONI MITCHELL

138

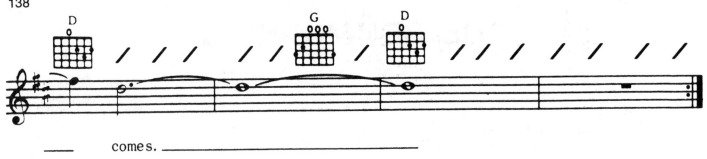

comes.

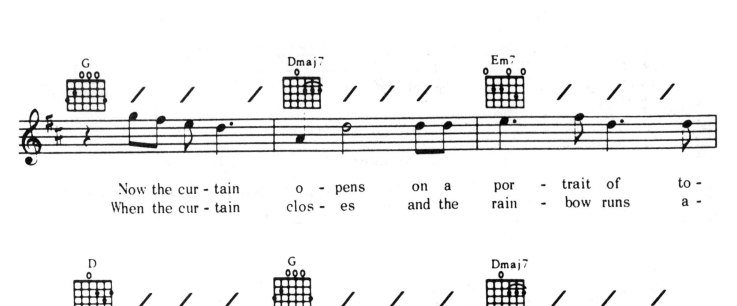

Now the cur - tain   o - pens   on a   por - trait of   to -
When the cur - tain   clos - es   and the   rain - bow runs   a -

day,   and the   streets are   paved with   pass - ers   by,   and
way,   I   will   bring you   in - cense owls   by   night,   by

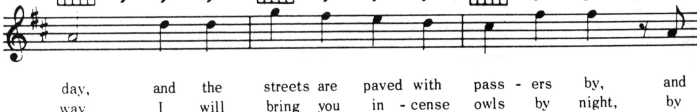

To Coda ⊕

pig - eons   fly___   and   pa - pers   lie_____   a - wait -
can - dle - light_   by   jew - el - light_____   if   on -

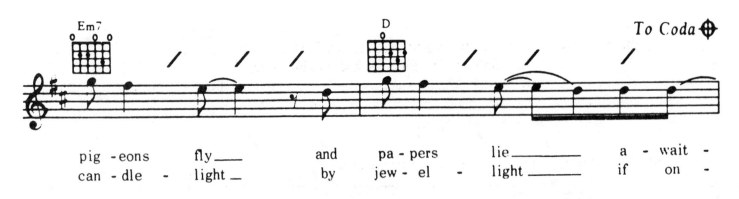

D. C. (no repeats) al Coda ⊕

ing   to blow_____   a - way._____

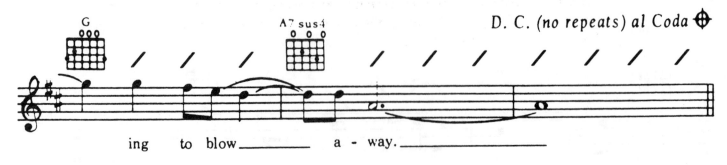

Coda

ly   you   will _____   stay. _____   Pret - ty

ba - by,   won't   you   wake up __   it's   a   Chel - sea __ morn -

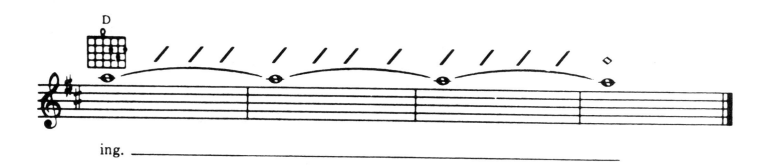

ing. _____

2. Woke up it was a Chelsea morning and the first thing that I saw
   Was the sun through yellow curtains and a rainbow on my wall.
   Blue, red, green and gold to welcome you, crimson crystal beads to beckon.
   Oh, won't you stay, we'll put on the day, there's a sun show every second.
   Now the curtain opens *(etc.)*

3. Woke up it was a Chelsea morning and the first thing that I knew,
   There was milk and toast and honey, and a bowl of oranges, too.
   And the sun poured in like butterscotch and stuck to all my senses.
   Oh, won't you stay, we'll put on the day and we'll talk in present tenses.
   When the curtain closes *(etc.)*

MR. BOJANGLES

Words and Music by
JERRY JEFF WALKER

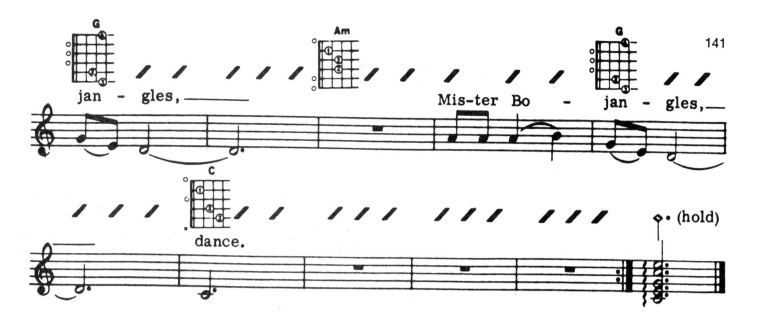

jan - gles, ———— Mis-ter Bo - jan - gles,——

dance. ———— ♩• (hold)

ADDITIONAL WORDS

2. I met him in a cell in New Orleans
   I was down and out.
   He looked at me to be the eyes of age,
   As he spoke right out.
   He talked of life,
   Talked of life.
   He laughed, slapped his leg a step.
   Mr. Bojangles, (etc.)

3. He said his name, Bojangles,
   Then he danced a lick across the cell.
   He grabbed his pants a better stance,
   Oh, he jumped up high,
   He clicked his heels.
   He let go a laugh,
   Let go a laugh,
   Shook back his clothes all around.
   Mr. Bojangles, (etc.)

4. He danced for those at minstrel shows
   And county fairs throughout the South.
   He spoke with tears of fifteen years
   How his dog and he traveled about.
   His dog up and died,
   He up and died,
   After twenty years he still grieved.
   Mr. Bojangles, (etc.)

5. He said, "I dance now at ev'ry chance
   In honky tonks for drinks and tips.
   But most of the time I spend
   Behind these county bars,"
   He said, "I drinks a bit."
   He shook his head and as he shook his head,
   I heard someone ask please,
   Mr. Bojangles, (etc.)

SOUTHERN NIGHTS

Words and Music by
ALLEN TOUSSAINT

SHE LOVES YOU

Words and Music by
JOHN LENNON and PAUL McCARTNEY

3. You know it's up to you,
   I think it's only fair,
   Pride can hurt you too,
   Apologize to her.
   Because she loves you, and you know that can't be bad.
   Yes, she loves you, and you know you should be glad.
   She loves you *(etc.)*

WOODSTOCK

Words and Music by
JONI MITCHELL

Suggested right hand pattern:

Moderately slow

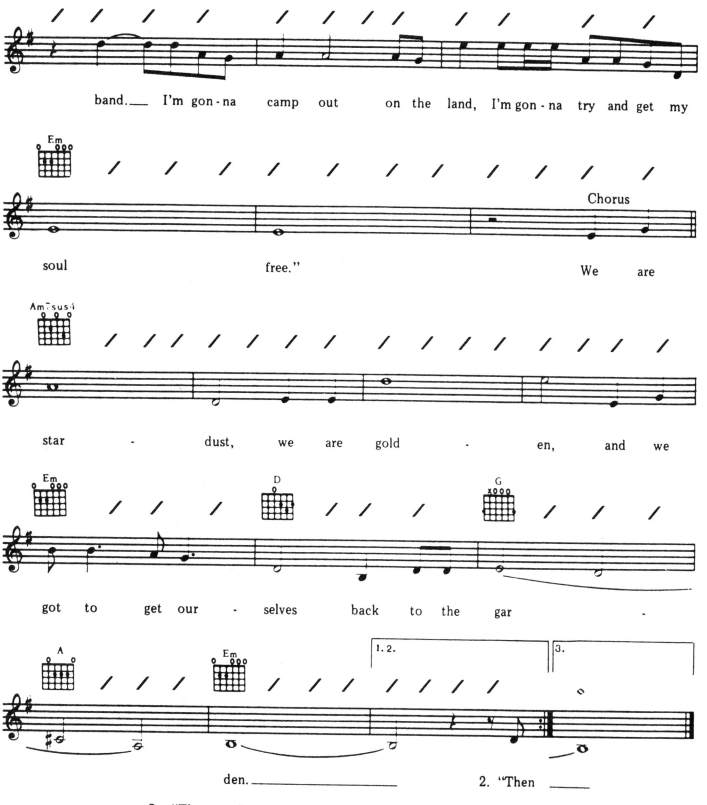

band.___ I'm gon-na camp out on the land, I'm gon-na try and get my

Em

Chorus

soul free." We are

Am⁷sus4

star - dust, we are gold - en, and we

Em   **D**   **G**

got to get our - selves back to the gar

A   **Em**   1. 2.   3.

den._____ 2. "Then _____

2. "Then can I walk beside you? I have come here to lose the smog,
   And I feel to be a cog in something turning.
   Well, maybe it is just the time of year, or maybe it's the time of man.
   I don't know who I am, but life is for learning."
   (Chorus)

3. By the time we got to Woodstock we were half a million strong,
   And everywhere was song and celebration.
   And I dreamed I saw the bombers riding shotgun in the sky,
   And they were turning into butterflies above our nation.
   (Chorus)

LIFE IN THE FAST LANE

Words and Music by
DON HENLEY,
GLENN FREY and JOE WALSH

Moderate Rock beat

1. He was a hard-head-ed man.___ He was bru-tal-ly hand-some, and she was ter-mi-nal-ly pret-ty. She held him up, and he held her for ran-som in the heart_ of the cold, cold cit-y. He had a nas-ty rep-u-ta-tion as a cru-el dude._ They said he was ruth-less; they said he was crude.___ They had one thing in com-mon: they were good in bed._ She'd say, "Fast-er, fast-er. The lights are turn-ing red."_

Life in the fast lane   sure-ly make you lose your mind._   Life in the fast lane.

1.

2. Life in the fast lane; ev-'ry-thing, all the time._ Life in the fast lane, uh huh._

3. Life in the fast lane; ev-'ry-thing, all the time. Life in the fast lane, uh huh._

E(hold)   D/E(hold)   C/E(hold)

Life in the fast lane.   *Repeat and fade*   Life in the

A/E(hold)   E

fast lane.

2. Eager for action and hot for the game,
   The coming attraction, the drop of a name.
   They knew all the right people; they took all the right pills.
   They threw outrageous parties; they paid heavily bills.
   There were lines on the mirror, lines on her face.
   She pretended not to notice; she was caught up in the race.
   Out every evenin' until it was light,
   He was too tired to make it; she was too tired to fight about it.
   Life in the fast lane *(etc.)*

3. Blowin' and burnin', blinded by thirst,
   They didn't see the stop sign; took a turn for the worst.
   She said, "Listen, baby. You can hear the engine ring.
   We've been up and down this highway; haven't seen a god-damn thing."
   He said, "Call the doctor. I think I'm gonna crash."
   "The doctor say he's comin', but you gotta pay him cash."
   They went rushin' down that freeway; messed around and got lost.
   They didn't know they were just dyin' to get off.
   And it was life in the fast lane *(etc.)*

AFTER THE THRILL IS GONE

Words and Music by
DON HENLEY and GLENN FREY

151

HEART OF GOLD

Words and Music by
NEIL YOUNG

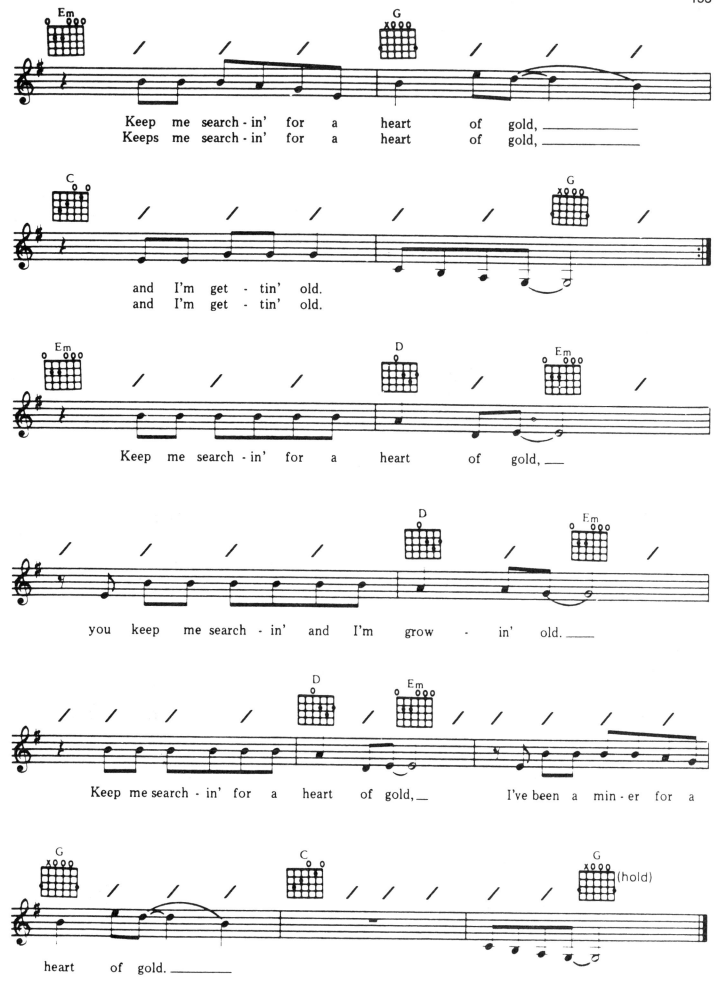

STILL THE SAME

Words and Music by
BOB SEGER

155

no one stand-in' in your way.— Turn-in' on the charm—

— long e-nough to get you by.————

You're still the same.—— You still aim

high.——————— And you're still the same.—

And you're still the same.—

Additional lyrics

2. You always said the cards would never do you wrong.
   The trick, you said, was never play the game too long.
   A gambler's share; the only risk that you would take,
   The only loss you could forsake,
   The only bluff you couldn't fake.

Bridge

3. *Instrumental*————————————

There you stood; everybody watched you play.
I just turned and walked away.
I had nothing left to say.

TAKE IT EASY

Words and Music by
JACKSON BROWNE and GLENN FREY

Moderate Country style

1. Well, I'm a - run-nin' down the road try'n' to loos-en my load, I've got

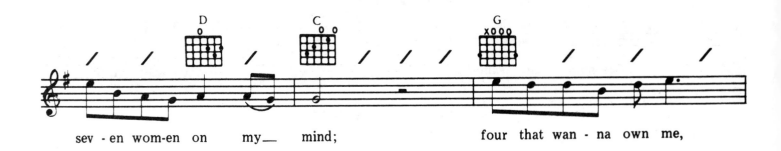

sev-en wom-en on my __ mind; four that wan-na own me,

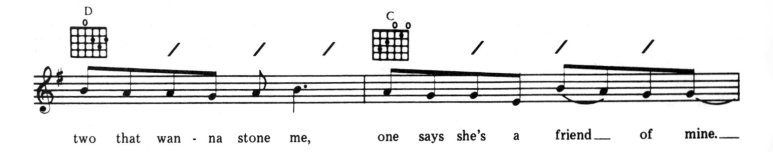

two that wan-na stone me, one says she's a friend __ of mine. __

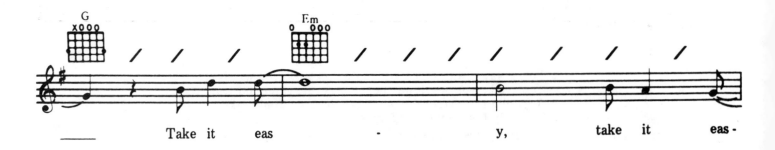

__ Take it eas - y, take it eas-

y, don't let the sound of your __ own

2. Well, I'm a-standin' on a corner in Winslow, Arizona, and such a fine sight to see,
It's a girl, my Lord, in a flat-bed Ford slowin' down to take a look at me.
Come on, baby, don't say maybe,
I gotta know if your sweet love is gonna save me.
We may lose and we may win, though we will never be here again,
So open up, I'm climbin' in, so take it easy.

3. Well, I'm a-runnin' down the road tryin' to loosen my load, got a world of trouble on my mind,
Lookin' for a lover who won't blow my cover, she's so hard to find.
Take it easy, take it easy.
Don't let the sound of your own wheels make you crazy.
Come on baby, don't say maybe,
I gotta know if your sweet love is gonna save me.

THAT GIRL COULD SING

Words and Music by
JACKSON BROWNE

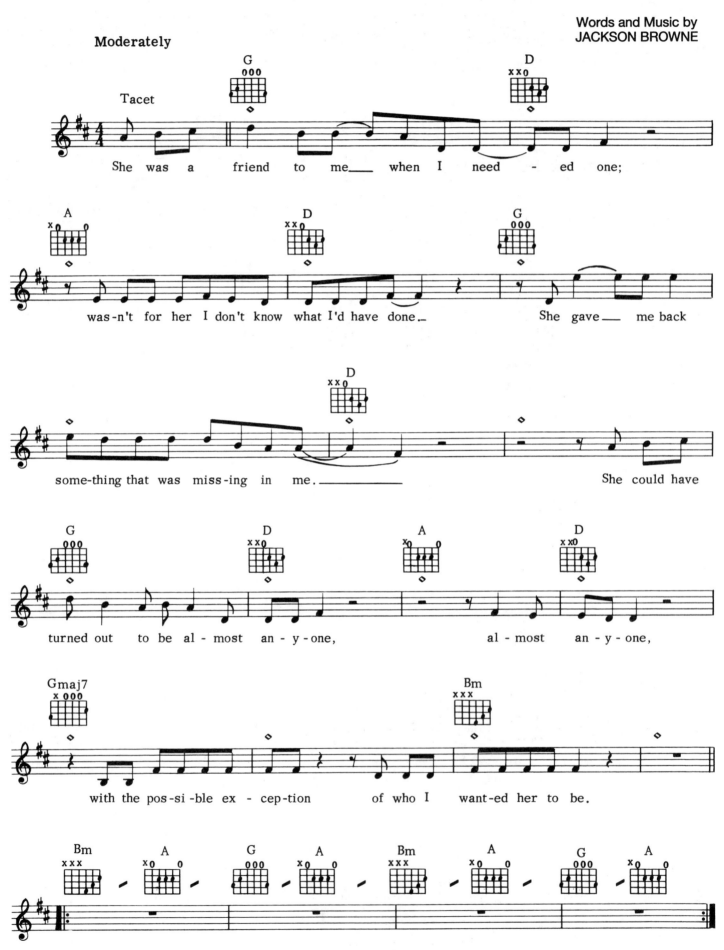

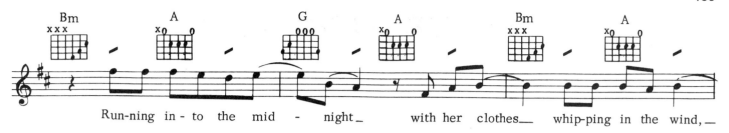

Run-ning in - to the mid - night__ with her clothes__ whip-ping in the wind,__

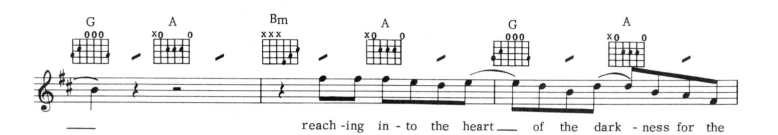

__ reach-ing in - to the heart__ of the dark - ness for the

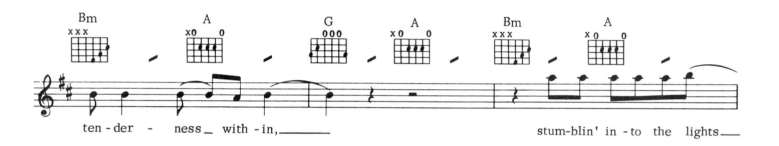

ten - der - ness__ with -in,_____ stum-blin' in -to the lights__

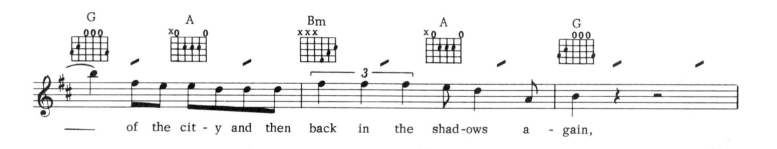

__ of the cit - y and then back in the shad-ows a - gain,

hang-ing on - to the laugh - ter that each of us hid our un - hap - pi -ness

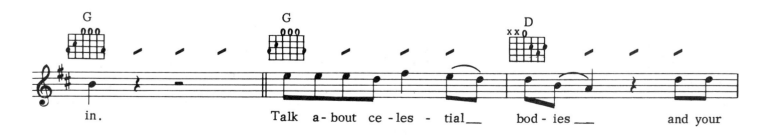

in. Talk a-bout ce - les - tial__ bod - ies __ and your

UNDERCOVER ANGEL

Words and Music by
ALAN O' DAY

Love me, love_ me, love_____ me.

Additional lyrics

2. Heavenly surrender, sweet afterglow.
   I've given up my heart to you. Now, angel, don't go.
   She said, "Go find the right one; love her and then
   When you look into her eyes, you'll see me again."
   I said, "What?" She said, "Ooo wee."
   I said, "All right!" She said, "Love me, love me, love me."

3. Now you know my story. And girl, if it's alright
   I'm gonna take you in my arms and love you tonight.
   Underneath the colors the answer lies
   I'm looking for my angel in your sweet lovin' eyes.
   She said, "What?" I said, "Ooo wee."
   She said, "All right!" I said, "Love me, love me, love me."

MY SHARONA

Words and Music by
DOUG FIEGER and BERTON AVERRE

Nev - er gon - na stop; give it up. Such a dirt - y mind. I

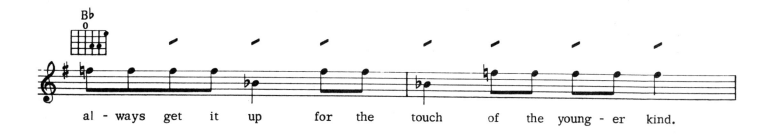

al - ways get it up for the touch of the young - er kind.

My, my, __ my, _____ yi, yi, whoo! M - m - m -

1.

(guitar)

my Sha - ro - na.

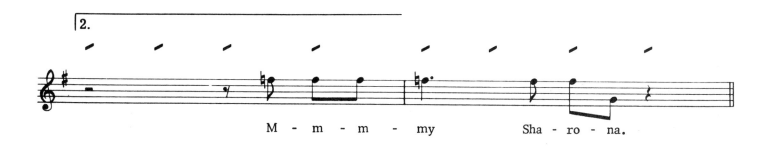

2.

M - m - m - my Sha - ro - na.

WARM LOVE

Moderately slow

Words and Music by
VAN MORRISON

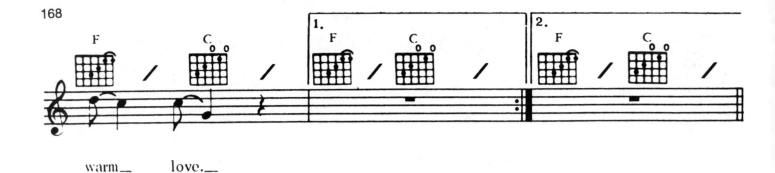

warm___ love.___

Chorus

And it's ev-er-pres-ent ev-'ry-where,   and it's ev-er-pres-ent ev-'ry-where, that

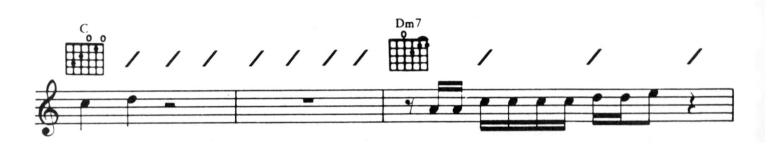

warm love.   And it's ev-er-pres-ent ev-'ry-where,

To Coda ⊕

and it's ev-er-pres-ent ev-'ry-where, that   warm   love.

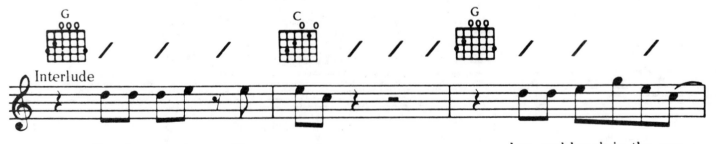

Interlude

To the coun-try   I'm   go-ing,   lay and laugh in the sun.___

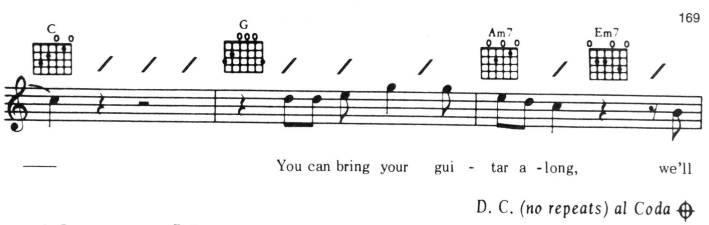

You can bring your gui - tar a -long, we'll

D. C. *(no repeats) al Coda* ⊕

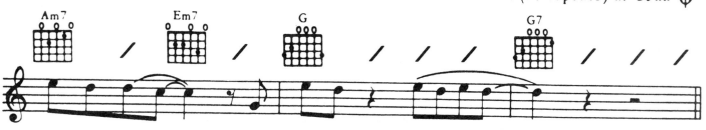

sing some songs____ and have some fun. _____

Coda
⊕

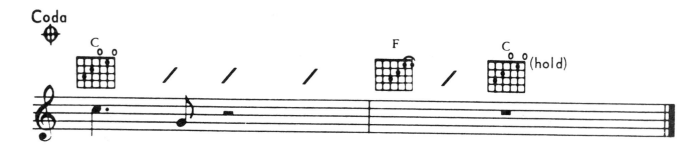

warm love.

Verse 2. I dig it when you're fancy, dressed up in lace,
I dig it when you have a smile on your face.
This inspiration's got to be on the flow,
This invitation's got to see it and know.
It's just warm love,
It's just warm love.
(Chorus and Interlude)

Verse 3. The sky is crying and it's time to go home,
And we shall hurry to the car from the foam.
Sit by the fire and dry out our wet clothes,
It's raining outside from the skies up above.
Inside it's warm love,
Inside it's warm love.
(Chorus)

Too Much, Too Little, Too Late

Words and Music by
NAT KIPNER and JOHN VALLINS

Additional lyrics

Guess it's over. The chips are down.
Pity all our bridges tumbled down.
Whatever chance we try,
Let's face it, why deny it's over, it's over.

CHINA GROVE

Words and Music by
TOM JOHNSTON

HOTEL CALIFORNIA

Words and Music by
DON HENLEY,
GLENN FREY and DON FELDER

175

SHAKE IT UP

Words and Music by
RIC OCASEK

Dance all night. Play all day. __
Dance all night. Get real loose. __

Don't let noth - ing get in the way. __
You don't need no bad __ ex - cuse. __

Dance all night. Keep the beat. __
Dance all night with an - y - one. __

Don't you wor - ry 'bout two left feet. __ } Just shake it
Don't let no - bod - y pick your fun. __

up. Shake it up. Shake it

up. Shake it up.

Dance all night. Go, go, go. —

Dance all night. Get real low. Go all night.

Get real hot. — Shake it up with all you got.

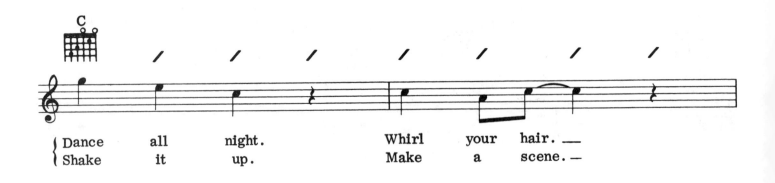

Dance all night. Whirl your hair. —
Shake it up. Make a scene. —

Make the night cats stop and stare. —
Let 'em know what you real - ly mean. —

Dance   all   night.   Go   to   work.—
Dance   all   night.   Keep   the   beat.—

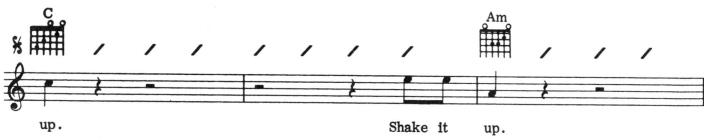

Do   the   move   with   the   quirk - y   jerk.—} Just shake it
Don't you wor - ry 'bout   two   left   feet.—

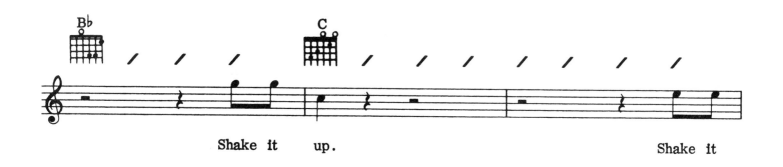

up.   Shake it   up.

Shake it   up.   Shake it

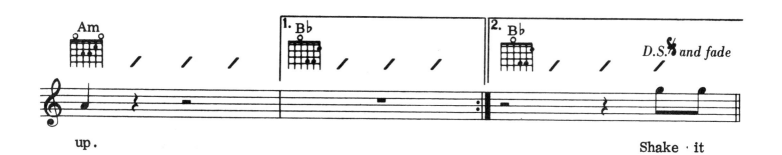

up.   Shake · it

FOLLOW YOU, FOLLOW ME

By
TONY BANKS,
PHIL COLLINS and MIKE RUTHERFORD

THE SPIRIT OF RADIO

Words by
NEIL PEART

Music by
GEDDY LEE and ALEX LIFESON

184

THAT'S ALL

By
TONY BANKS,
PHIL COLLINS and **MIKE RUTHERFORD**

I could leave but I ___ won't go, though ___ my heart might tell me so. ___ I can't feel a thing ___ from my head down to my toes. So why does it al - ways seem to be me look-ing at you, ___ you ___ look-ing at me. S'al - ways the same; ___ it's just a shame, that's all. _____ 2. Turn-ing me on, ___

Truth is _____ I love you ___

Verse 2. Turning me on, turning me off,
Making me feel like I want too much.
Living with you's just putting me through it all of the time.
Running around, staying out all night,
Taking it all 'stead of taking one bite.
Living with you's just putting me through it all of the time.

Chorus II. I could leave but I won't go.
It'd be easier, I know.
I can't feel a thing from my head down to my toes.
But why does it always seem to be
Me looking at you, you looking at me.
S'always the same; it's just a shame, that's all.

Bridge

Verse 3. *Repeat Verse 1.*

A HORSE WITH NO NAME

Words and Music by
DEWEY BUNNELL

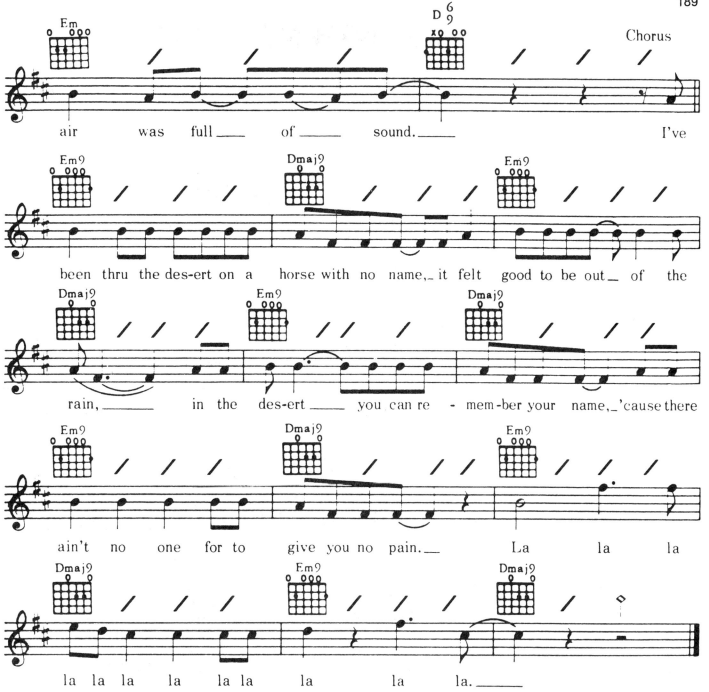

2. After nine days I let the horse run free 'cause the desert had turned to sea,
There were plants and birds and rocks and things, there were sand and hills and rings.
The ocean is a desert with its life underground and the perfect disguise above,
Under the cities lies a heart made of ground, but the humans will give no love.
(Chorus)

3. After two days in the desert sun my skin began to turn red,
After three days in the desert fun I was looking at a river bed.
And the story it told of a river that flowed made me sad to think it was dead.
(Chorus)

RAINY DAY PEOPLE

Words and Music by
GORDON LIGHTFOOT

1. Rain - y day peo - ple al - ways seem to know when it's

time to call; ___ rain - y day peo - ple don't

talk, they just lis - ten till they've heard it all. ___

Rain - y day lov - ers don't lie when they tell ya

they bin down like you; ___

rain - y day peo - ple don't mind if you're cry - in' a

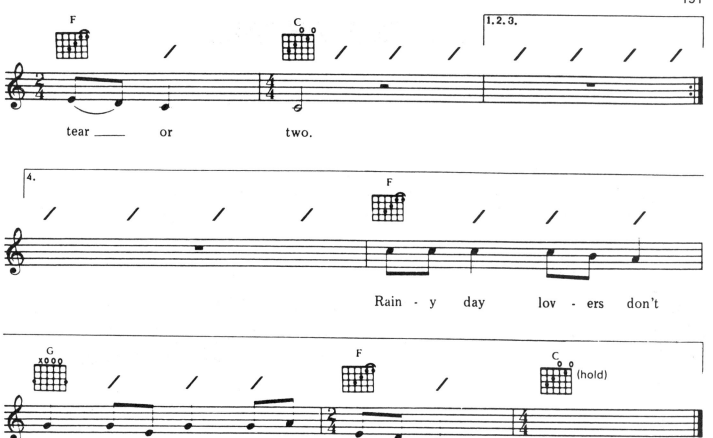

tear ___ or two.

Rain - y day lov - ers don't

hide love in - side, they just pass ___ it on.

2. If you get lonely all you really need is that rainy day love;
   Rainy day people all know there's no sorrow they can't rise above.
   Rainy day lovers don't love any others, that would not be kind;
   Rainy day people all know how it hangs on your peace of mind.

3. *Instrumental* _____

   Rainy day lovers don't lie when they tell ya they bin down there too;
   Rainy day people don't mind if you're cryin' a tear or two.

4. Rainy day people always seem to know when you're feelin' blue;
   High-steppin' strutters who land in the gutter sometimes need one too.
   Take it or leave it or try to believe it if you bin down too long;
   Rainy day lovers don't hide love inside, they just pass it on.
   Rainy day lovers don't hide love inside, they just pass it on.

SOUTHERN MAN

Words and Music by
NEIL YOUNG

COUNTRY GIRL

Words and Music by
NEIL YOUNG

CIRCLE OF STEEL

Words and Music by
GORDON LIGHTFOOT

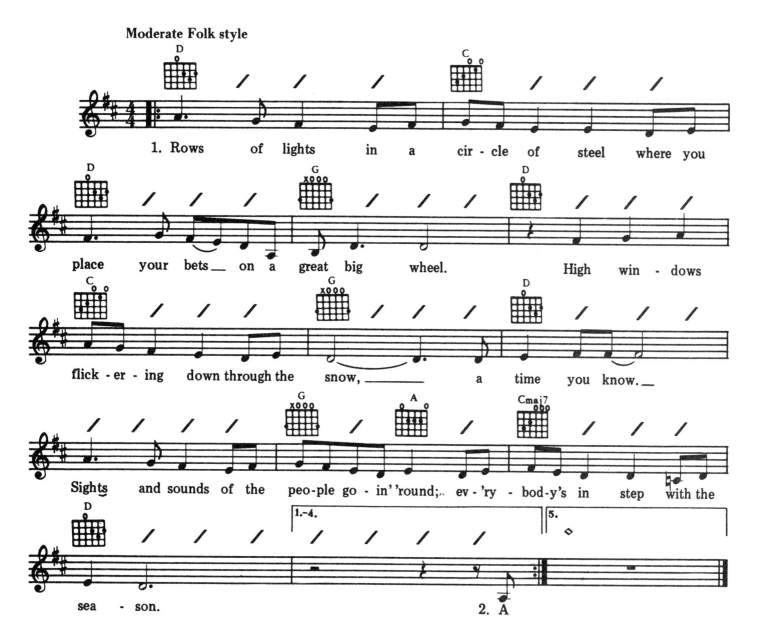

Moderate Folk style

1. Rows of lights in a cir-cle of steel where you place your bets on a great big wheel. High win-dows flick-er-ing down through the snow, a time you know. Sights and sounds of the peo-ple go-in' 'round; ev-'ry-bod-y's in step with the sea-son.

2. A child is born to a welfare case where the rats run around like they own the place.
   The room is chilly, the building is old; that's how it goes.
   A doctor's found on his welfare rounds, and he comes and he leaves on the double.

3. "Deck the Halls" was the song they played in the flat next door where they shout all day.
   She tips her gin bottle back till it's gone; the child is strong.
   A week, a day, they will take it away for they know about all her bad habits.

4. Christmas dawns and the snow lets up, and the sun hits the handle of her heirloom cup.
   She hides her face in her hands for a while, says, "Look here, child,
   Your father's pride was his means to provide, and he's serving three years for that reason."

5. *(Repeat Verse 1)*

HELPLESS

Words and Music by
NEIL YOUNG

Moderately slow

There is a town in north On - tar - i - o

with dream com-fort mem-o - ry to spare;   and in my mind   I still

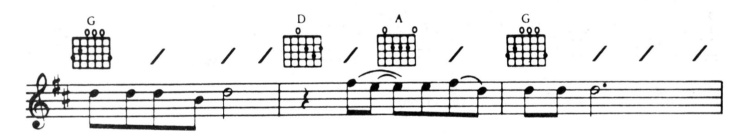

need a place to go,   all ____ my chang - es were there.

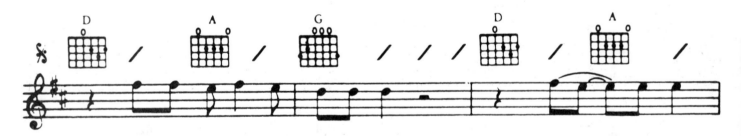

Blue, blue win-dows be - hind the stars,   yel - low moon

on the rise;   big birds fly - ing a - cross the sky

199

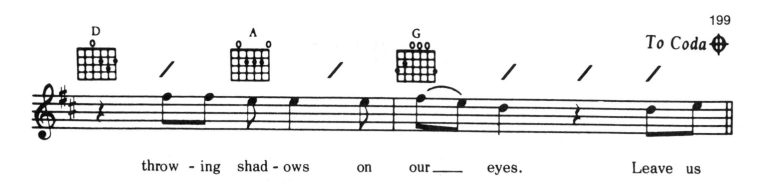

throw - ing shad - ows   on   our___ eyes.   Leave us

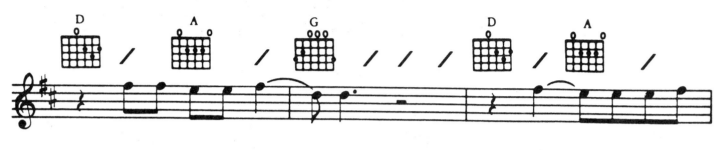

help-less, help-less,help - less,   ba - by can you

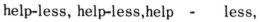

hear me now?   The chains___ are locked and   tied a-cross the door,

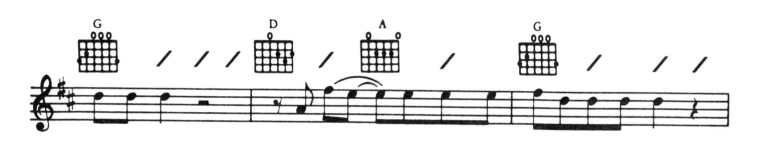

D. S. %&al Coda⊕

ba - by   sing_____ with me some-how.

Coda
⊕
Repeat and fade

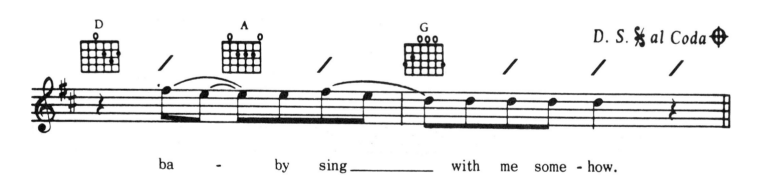

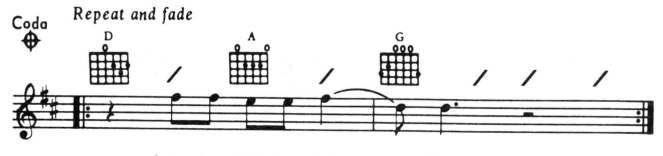

help - less, help-less, help - less.

CHRISTIAN ISLAND

(Georgian Bay)

Words and Music by
GORDON LIGHTFOOT

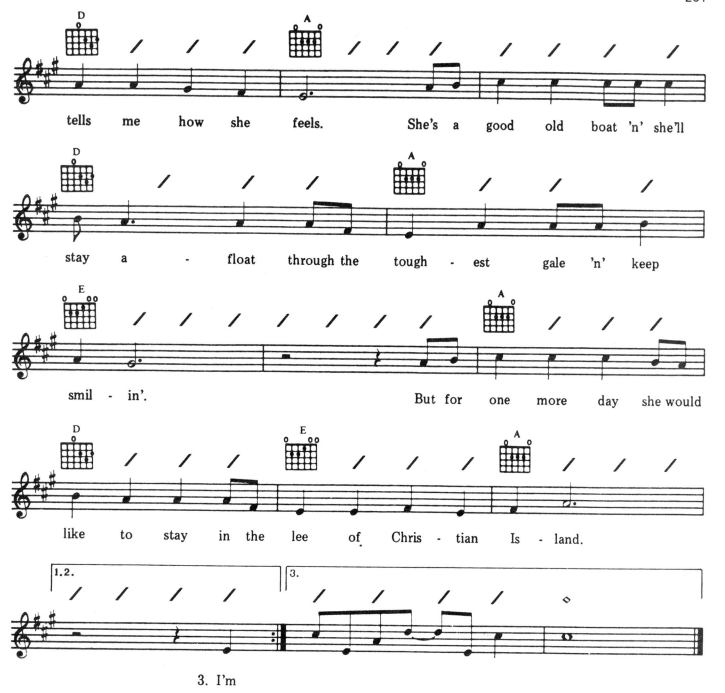

tells me how she feels. She's a good old boat 'n' she'll

stay a - float through the tough - est gale 'n' keep

smil - in'. But for one more day she would

like to stay in the lee of Chris - tian Is - land.

3. I'm

3. I'm sailin' down the summer day
   Where fish and seagulls play; I put my troubles all away.
   And when the gale comes up I'll fill my cup with the whiskey of the Highlands.
   She's a good old ship 'n' she'll make the trip from the lee of Christian Island.

4. Tall and strong she slips along,
   I sing for her a song and she leans into the wind.
   She's a good old boat 'n' she'll stay afloat through the toughest gale 'n' keep smilin'.
   When the summer ends we will rest again in the lee of Christian Island.

VENTURA HIGHWAY

Words and Music by
DEWEY BUNNELL

Moderately

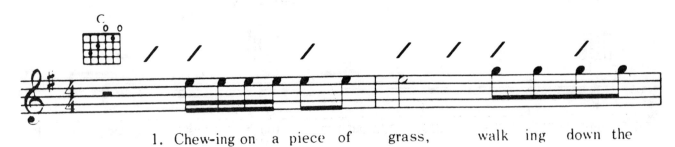

1. Chew-ing on a piece of grass, walk ing down the

road. ____

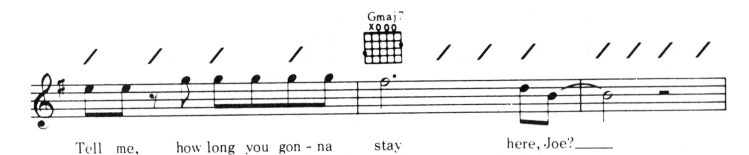

Tell me, how long you gon - na stay here, Joe? ____

Some peo-ple say this town don't look good in snow, ____

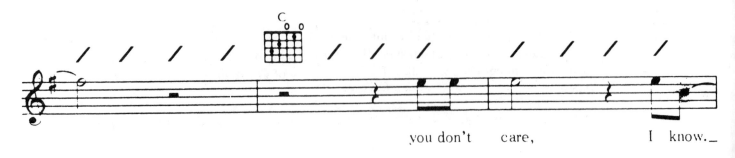

you don't care, I know. ____

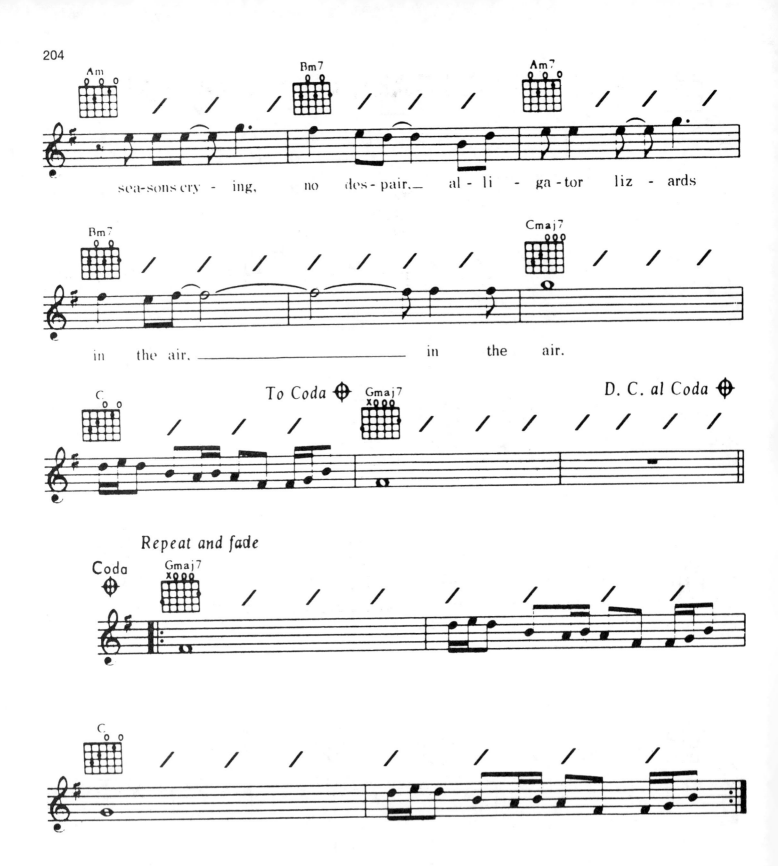

sea-sons cry - ing, no des - pair,_ al - li - ga - tor liz - ards

in the air. _____ in the air.

To Coda ⊕   D. C. al Coda ⊕

Repeat and fade

Coda ⊕

2. Wishin' on a falling star, waiting for the early train,
   Sorry, boy, but I've been hit by purple rain.
   Aw, come on, Joe, you can always change your name.
   Thanks a lot son, just the same.
   Ventura Highway *(etc.)*

WHENEVER I CALL YOU "FRIEND"

Words by
KENNY LOGGINS and MELISSA MANCHESTER

Music by
KENNY LOGGINS

SUMMER ME, WINTER ME
("PICASSO SUMMER")

Lyric by
MARILYN and ALAN BERGMAN

Music by
MICHEL LEGRAND

209

WELCOME BACK

Moderate shuffle beat

Words and Music by
JOHN SEBASTIAN

Wel-come back;_ your dreams were your tick-et out.___ Wel-come
back;_ You al-ways could spot a friend._ Wel-come

back_ to that same old place that you laughed a-bout. Well, the
back; and I smile when I think how you must have been. And I

names___ have all changed___ since you hung a-round, but those
know___ what a scene___ you were learn-in' in; was there

dreams_ have re-mained_ and they've turned a-round. Who'd have thought they'd lead ya
some-thing that made___ you come back a-gain? And what could ev-er lead ya

back here where we need ya?
back here where we need ya? Yeah, we tease him a lot_ 'cause we

got him on the spot; wel-come back.___ Wel-come back, wel-come back, wel-come

back.___ Wel-come back, wel-come back. Wel-come back, wel-come back, wel-come

back.___ Wel-come back, wel-come back, wel-come back.

REAL LOVE

Words and Music by
MICHAEL McDONALD and PATRICK HENDERSON

214

WOMAN TONIGHT

Words and Music by
DAN PEEK

HELP ME

Words and Music by
JONI MITCHELL

1. Help me, I think I'm fall-in' in love __ a - gain. __ When I get that cra - zy feel-in' I know I'm in trou-ble a - gain. __ I'm in trou - ble 'cause you're a ram - bler and a gam - bler and a sweet - talk - in' __ la - dies' man, and you love your

218

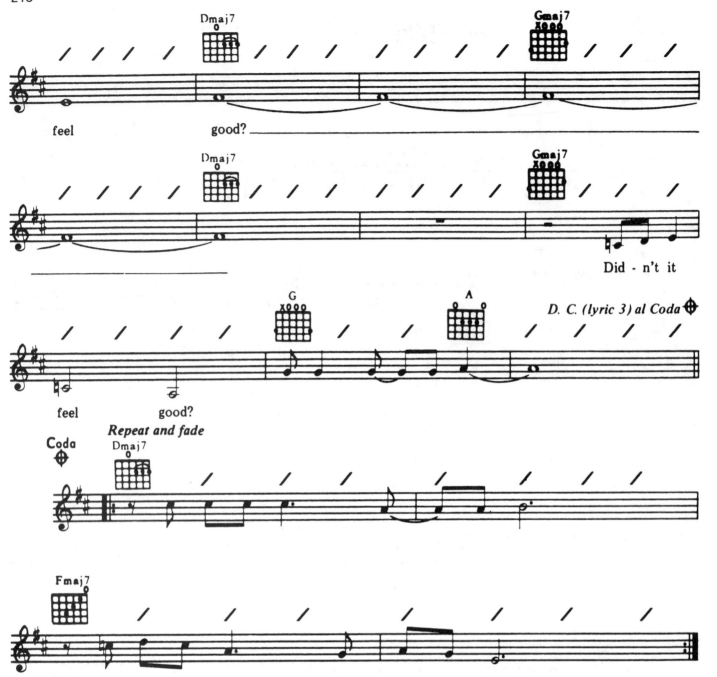

feel good?

Did - n't it

feel good?

2. Help me, I think I'm falling in love too fast.
   It's got me hoping for the future and worrying about the past.
   'Cause I've seen some hot, hot blazes come down to smoke and ash.
   We love our lovin',
   But not like we love our freedom.

3. Help me, I think I'm falling in love with you.
   Are you gonna let me go there by myself? That's such a lonely thing to do.
   Both of us flirting around, flirting and flirting, hurting too.
   We love our lovin',
   But not like we love our freedom.

AGAINST THE WIND

Words and Music by
BOB SEGER

Additional lyrics

2. And the years rolled slowly past.
   And I found myself alone,
   Surrounded by strangers I thought were my friends.
   I found myself further and further from my home,
   And I guess I lost my way.
   There were oh so many roads.
   I was livin' to run and runnin' to live.
   Never worried about payin', or even how much I owed.
   Movin' eight miles a minute for months at a time,
   Breakin' all of the rules that would bend,
   I began to find myself searchin',
   Searchin' for shelter again and again.
   Against the wind,
   Little somethin' against the wind.
   I found myself seekin' shelter against the wind.

3. *Instrumental* _____
   _____
   _____
   _____
   _____
   _____
   _____
   _____

Well, those drifter's days are past me now.
I've got so much more to think about:
Deadlines and commitments,
What to leave in, what to leave out.
Against the wind,
I'm still runnin' against the wind.
I'm older now, but still runnin' against the wind.
Well, I'm older now, and still runnin' against the wind,
Against the wind.

YOU DON'T MESS AROUND WITH JIM

Words and Music by
JIM CROCE

come to get my mon-ey back." And ev-'ry-bod-y say, "Jack, don't you

D.S. %̸ al Coda ⊕

know that you don't

Coda ⊕ Well, a hush fell o-ver the

pool-room, Jim-my come bop-pin' in off the street and when the

cut-tin' were done the on-ly part that was-n't blood-y was the

soles of the big man's feet. Yeah, he were cut in 'bout a hun-dred

pla-ces and he were shot in a cou-ple more and you

bet-ter be-lieve they sung a dif-f'rent kind of sto-ry when-a big Jim hit the

floor, oh. Now they say you don't

tug on Su-per-man's cape, you don't spit in-to the

wind,___ you don't pull the mask off the old Lone Rang-er and you

don't mess a-round with Slim.

1.

*(Spoken) Yeah big Jim got his hat; find **out** where it's at and not hustling people strange to you.*
Even if you do got a two-piece custom-made pool cue.

2.

Yeah, you don't tug on Su-per-man's cape, you don't

spit in-to the wind,___ you don't pull the mask off the

old Lone Rang-er and you don't mess a-round with Slim.

MONEY

Words and Music by
ROGER WATERS

EARLY MORNIN' RAIN

Words and Music by
GORDON LIGHTFOOT

Starting note for singing:

(N.C.) **Gmodal** / / / / / / **Cadd9** / / /

1. In the ear - ly morn - in' rain ____

Gmodal / / / **D7** / / / **G** / / / **C** / / /

with a dol - lar in my hand.

G / / / / / / **Am** / / / / / /

With an ach - in' in my heart

/ / / / / / **G** / / / / / /

and my pock - ets full of sand. ____

/ / / / / / **Am** / / / / / /

I'm a long way from home ____

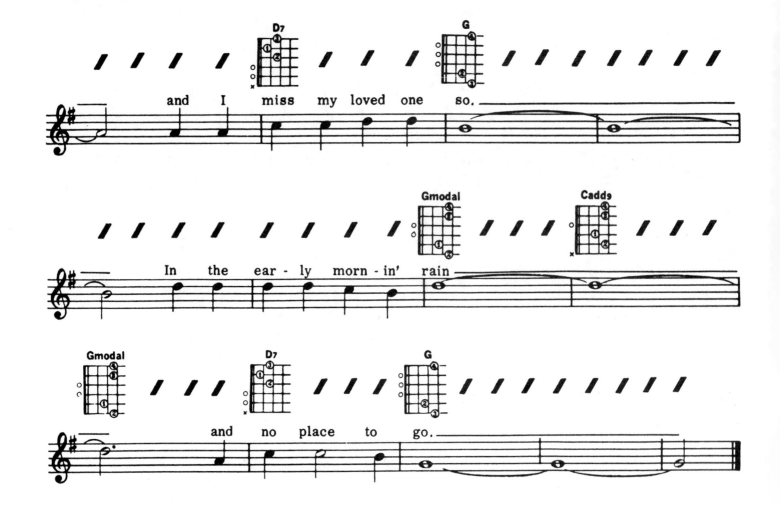

and I miss my loved one so.

In the ear-ly morn-in' rain

and no place to go.

2. Out on runway number nine
Big seven-o-seven set to go,
Well I'm standin' on the grass
Where the cold wind blows.
Well, the liquor tasted good
And the women all were fast,
Well, there she goes, my friend
There she's rollin' now at last.

3. Hear the mighty engines roar,
See the silver bird on high,
She's away and westward bound
Far above the clouds she'll fly,
Where the mornin' rain don't fall
And the sun always shines,
She'll be flyin' o'er my home
In about three hours time.

4. Well, this old airport's got me down,
It's no earthly good to me,
'Cause I'm stuck here on the ground
As cold and drunk as I can be.
You can't jump a jet plane
Like you can a freight train,
So I best be on my way
In the early mornin' rain.

DIXIELAND DELIGHT

Words and Music by
RONNIE ROGERS

Moderate Country style

TRYIN' TO GET THE FEELING AGAIN

Words and Music by
DAVID POMERANZ

TAKE IT TO THE LIMIT

Words and Music by
DON HENLEY,
GLENN FREY and RANDY MEISNER

234

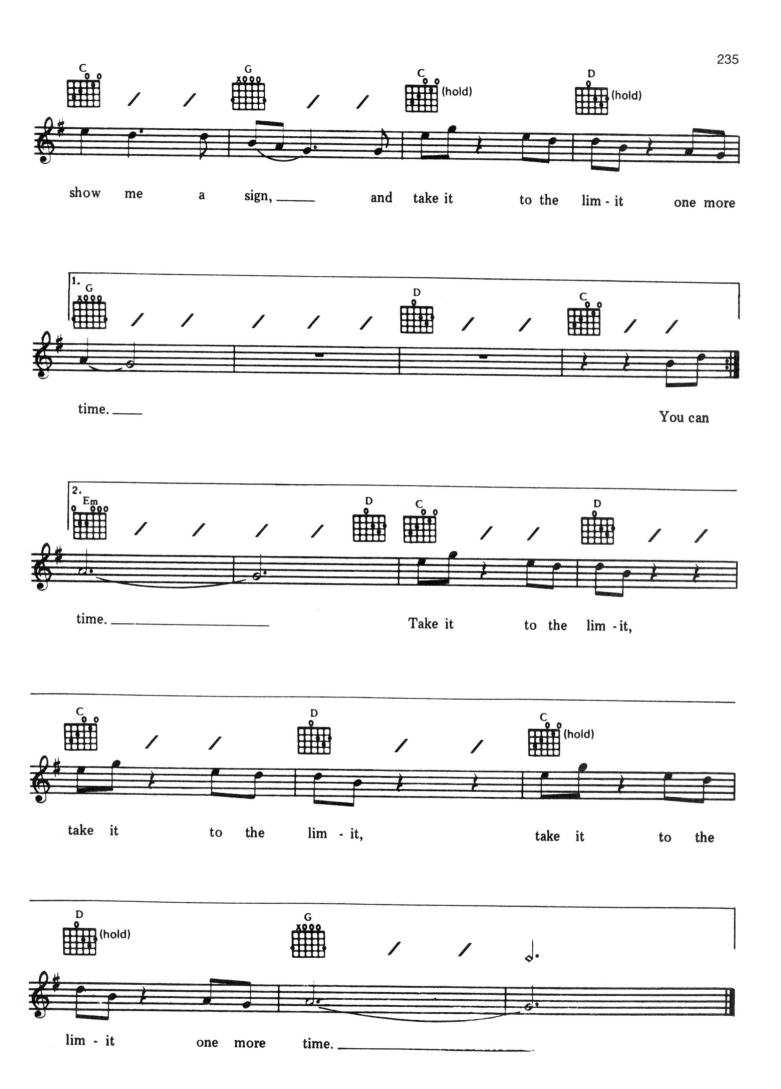

ROCKING PNEUMONIA
AND THE BOOGIE WOOGIE FLU

Words and Music by
HUEY SMITH

2. Want some loving, baby, that ain't all,
   I wanna kiss her but she's way too tall.
   Jump and rhythm's got a hold on me too,
   I've got the rocking pneumonia and the boogie-woogie flu.

3. Wanna squeeze her but I'm way too low,
   I would be running but my feet's too slow.
   Jump and rhythm's got a hold on me too,
   I've got the rocking pneumonia and the boogie-woogie flu.

4. Baby, coming now, I'm hurrying home,
   I know she'll leave me 'cause I'm taking too long.
   Jump and rhythm's got a hold on me too,
   I've got the rocking pneumonia and the boogie-woogie flu.

DON'T CRY

Words and Music by
JOHN WETTON and GEOFFREY DOWNES

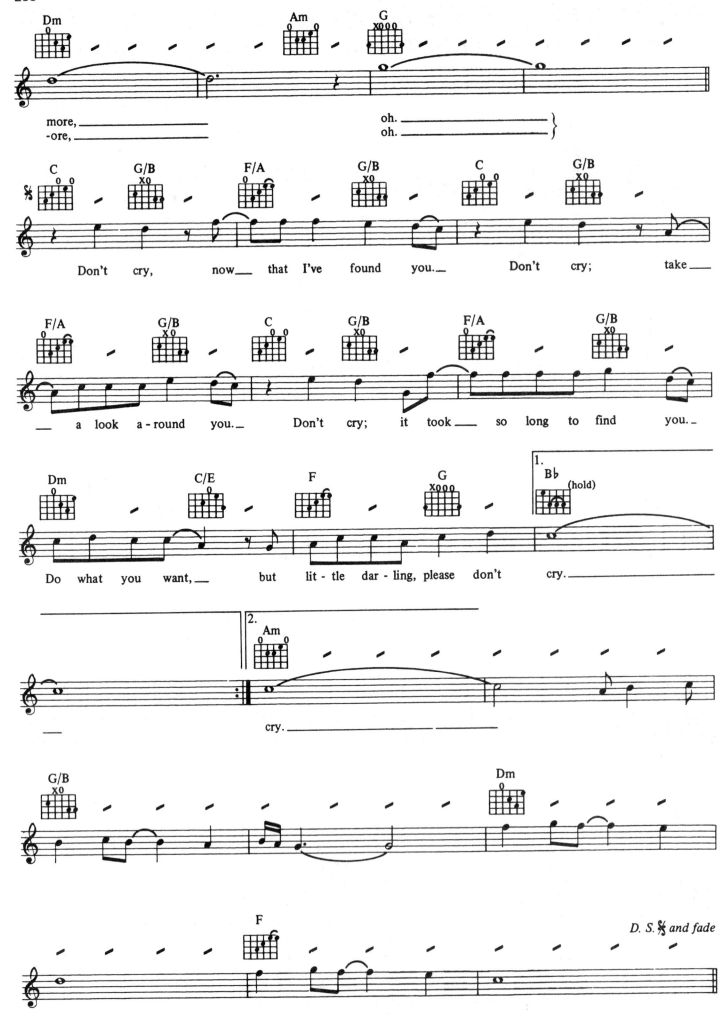

ARTHUR'S THEME (BEST THAT YOU CAN DO)
From "ARTHUR" an ORION PICTURES release through WARNER BROS.

Words and Music by
BURT BACHARACH, CAROLE BAYER SAGER,
CHRISTOPHER CROSS and PETER ALLEN

Once in your life you'll find_____ her,
Ar - thur, he does what he pleas - ses.

some - one who turns____ your heart a - round, and
All of his life,_____ his mas - ter's toys, and

next thing you know, you're clos - in'
deep in his heart, he's just he's

down the town. __
just a boy. __

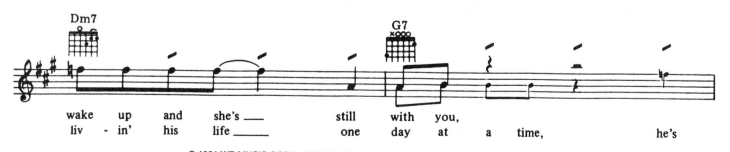

wake up and she's ____ still with you,
liv - in' his life _____ one day at a time, he's

240

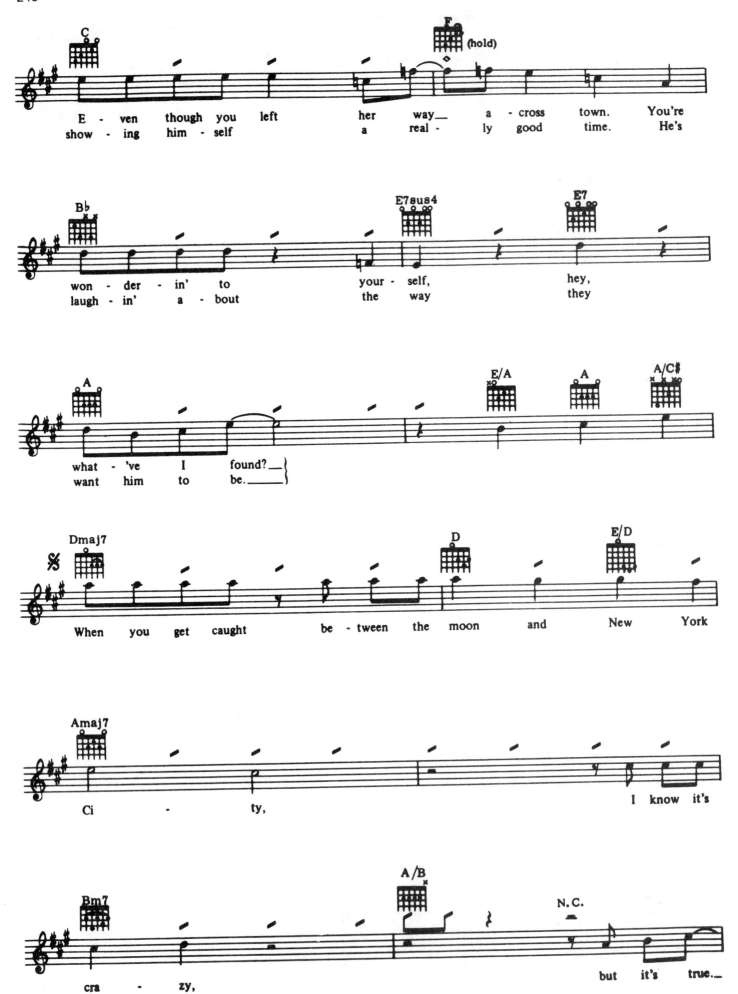

ESCAPE

(The Pina Colada Song)

Words and Music by
RUPERT HOLMES

Additional lyrics

2. I didn't think about my lady;
   I know that sounds kind of mean.
   But me and my old lady
   Have fallen into the same old dull routine.
   So I wrote to the paper,
   Took out a personal ad.
   And though I'm nobody's poet,
   I thought it wasn't half bad:
   "Yes, I like piña coladas
   And getting caught in the rain.
   I'm not much into health food;
   I am into champagne.
   I've got to meet you by tomorrow noon,
   And cut through all this red tape,
   At a bar called O'Malley's
   Where we'll plan our escape."

3. So I waited with high hopes
   And she walked in the place.
   I knew her smile in an instant.
   I knew the curve of her face.
   It was my lovely lady
   And she said, " Oh,it's you."
   Then we laughed for a moment
   And I said, " I never knew
   That you like piña coladas,
   Getting caught in the rain,
   And the feel of the ocean
   And the taste of champagne.
   If you'd like making love at midnight
   In the dunes on the Cape,
   You're the lady I've looked for.
   Come with me and escape."

LOTTA LOVE

Words and Music by
NEIL YOUNG

KARMA CHAMELEON

Words and Music by
PHIL PICKETT, GEORGE O'DOWD,
JON MOSS, MIKEY CRAIG and ROY HAY

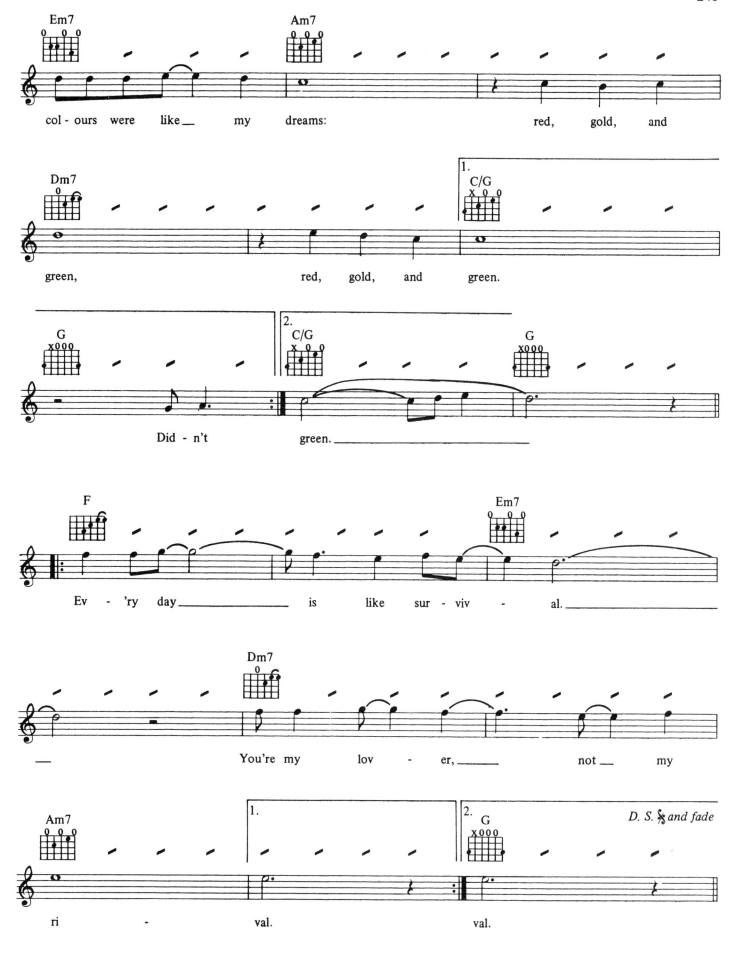

WE'VE GOT TONIGHT

Words and Music by
BOB SEGER

251

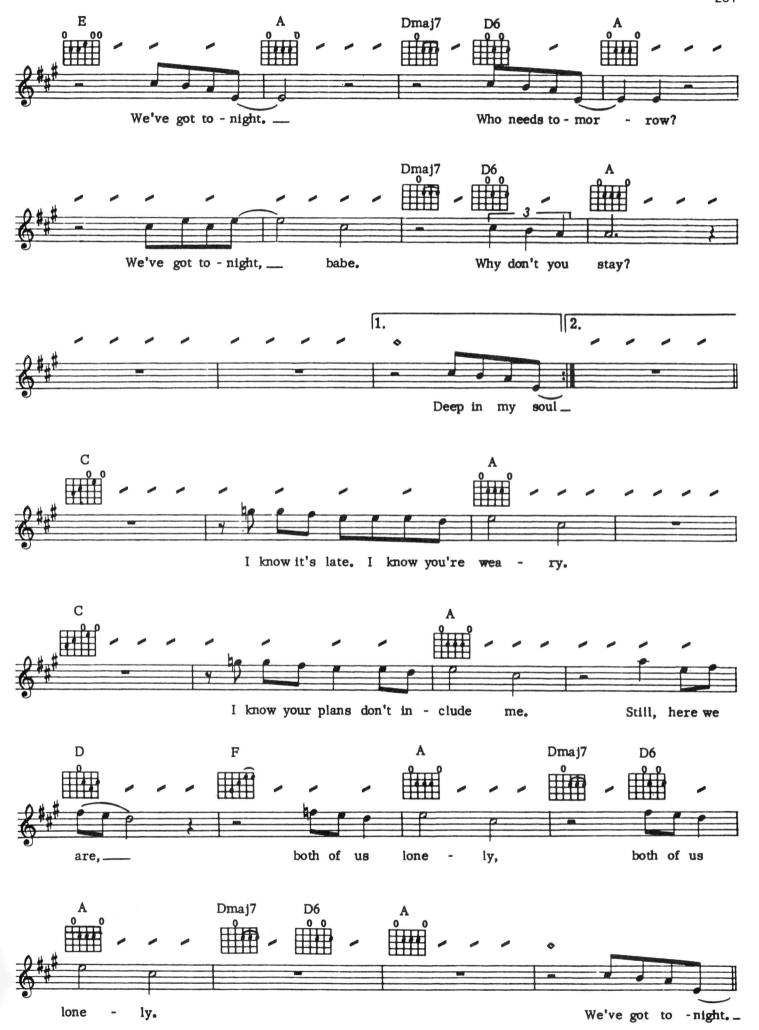

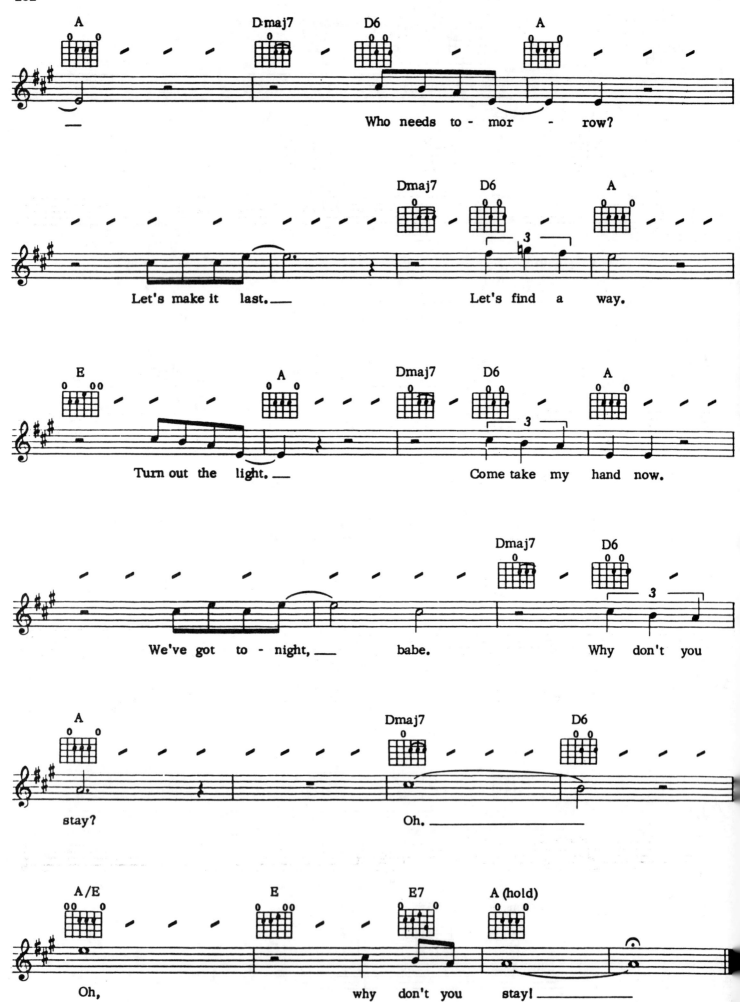

TUPELO HONEY

Words and Music by
VAN MORRISON

Slowly

Verse

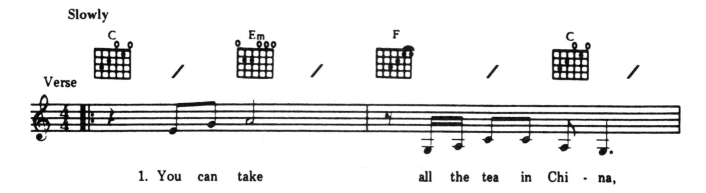

1. You can take all the tea in Chi - na,

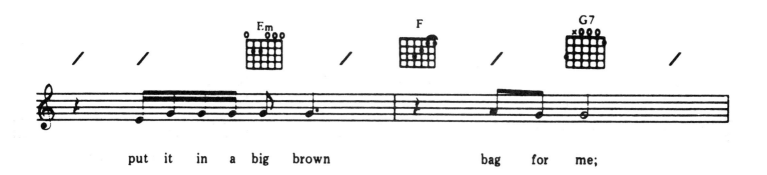

put it in a big brown bag for me;

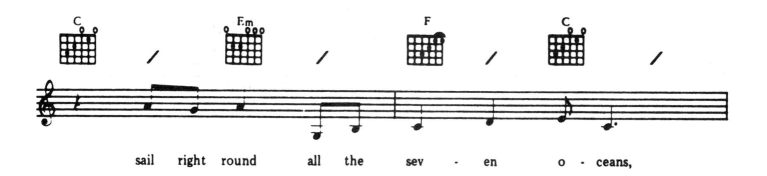

sail right round all the sev - en o - ceans,

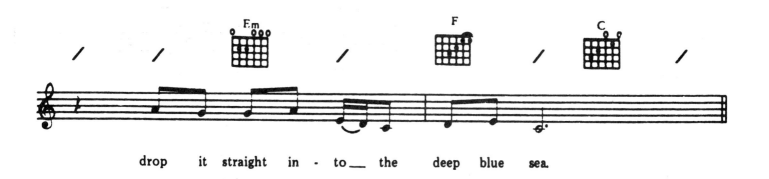

drop it straight in - to __ the deep blue sea.

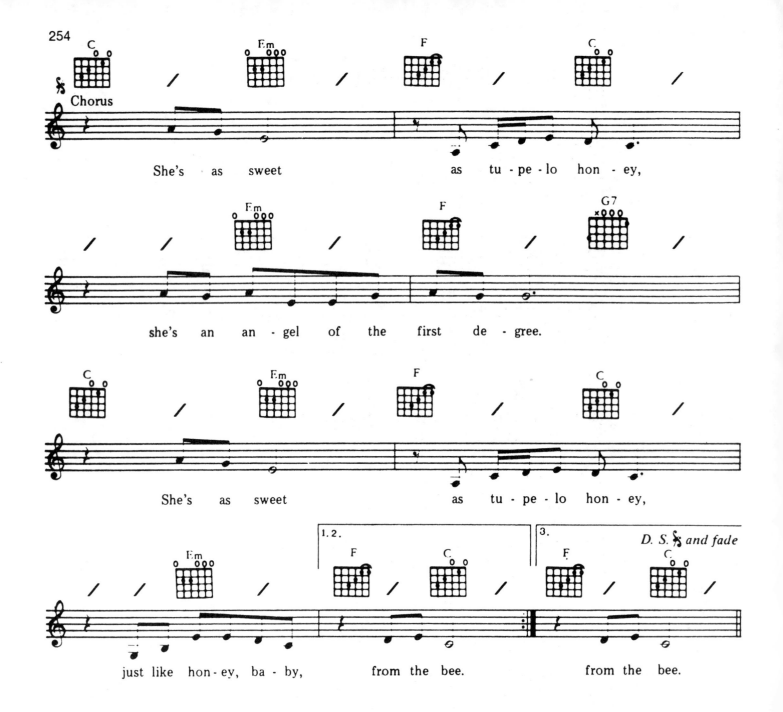

Chorus

She's as sweet as tu-pe-lo hon-ey,

she's an an-gel of the first de-gree.

She's as sweet as tu-pe-lo hon-ey,

just like hon-ey, ba-by, from the bee. from the bee.

1.2. 3. D. S. and fade

2. You can't stop us on the road to freedom;
   You can't keep us 'cause our eyes can see.
   Men with insight, men in granite,
   Knights in armour bent on chivalry.
   (Chorus)

3. I'll tell a tale of old Manhattan,
   Adirondack bus to go.
   Standing waiting on my number,
   And my number's gonna show.
   (Chorus)

DESPERADO

Words and Music by
DON HENLEY and GLENN FREY

seems to me some fine things have been laid up-on your ta-ble, but you

los-in' all your highs and lows. Ain't it fun-ny how the feel-in' goes a-

on-ly want the ones that you can't get. Des - per - way?

Des - per - a - do, why don't you come to your sens - es? Come

down from your fenc - es, o - pen the gate. It may be

rain - in', but there's a rain - bow a - bove you. You bet-ter

let some - bod - y love you, you bet - ter

let some - bod - y love you be - fore it's too late.

STAND BACK

Words and Music
STEVIE NICKS

258

TAKIN' IT TO THE STREETS

Words and Music by
MICHAEL McDONALD

Moderately fast

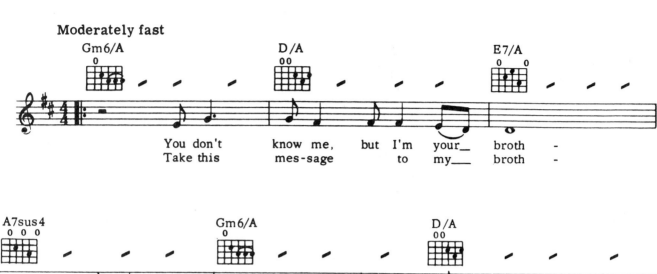

You don't know me, but I'm your broth -
Take this mes-sage to my broth -

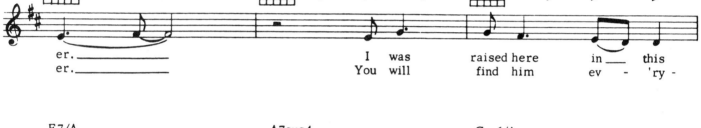

er. _____
er. _____   I was raised here in this
You will find him ev - 'ry -

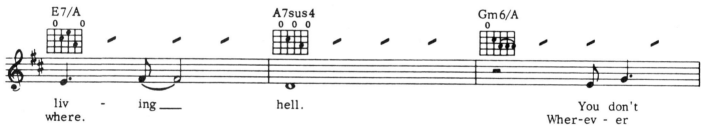

liv - ing _____ hell.   You don't
where.   Wher-ev - er

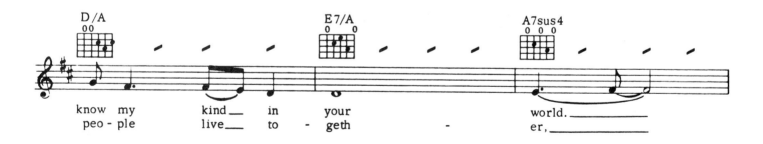

know my kind _____ in your world. _____
peo - ple kind live _____ to - geth - er, _____

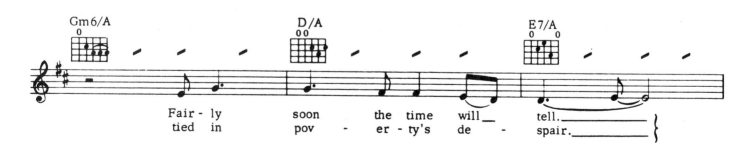

Fair - ly soon the time will _____ tell. _____
tied in pov - er - ty's de - spair. _____

260

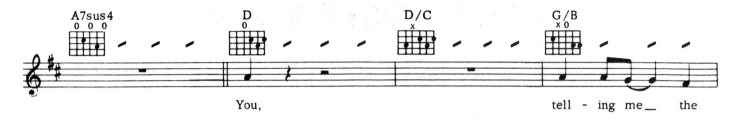

You,   tell - ing me __ the

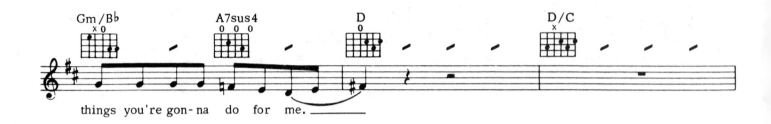

things you're gon- na do for me. _____

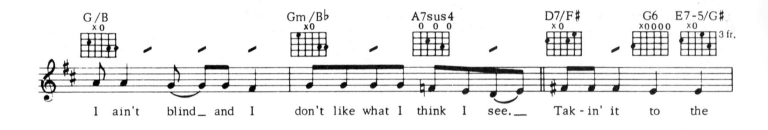

I ain't   blind _ and I   don't like what I think I see. __ Tak - in' it   to   the

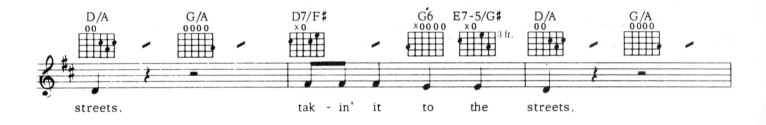

streets.   tak - in' it   to   the   streets,

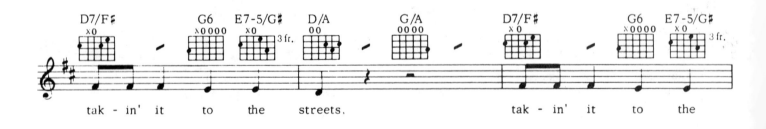

tak - in' it   to   the   streets,   tak - in' it   to   the

Repeat and fade

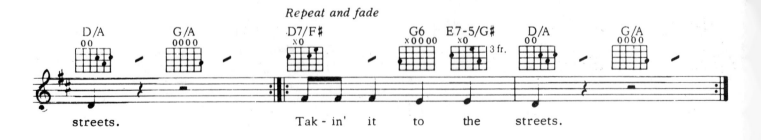

streets.   Tak - in' it   to   the   streets.

FOUR STRONG WINDS

Word and Music by
IAN TYSON

262

BOTH SIDES NOW

Words and Music by
JONI MITCHELL

1. Bows and flows of an-gel hair and ice-cream cas-tles

in the air,— and feath-er can-yons _____ ev-'ry-where,

I've looked at clouds that way. But now they on-ly

block the sun,— they rain and snow on ev-'ry-one.— So

man-y things I ____ would have done but clouds got in my

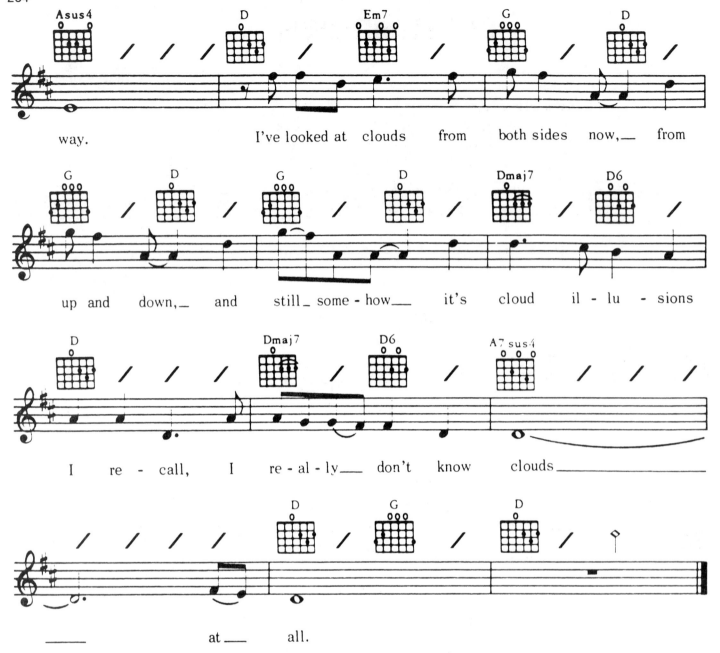

way. I've looked at clouds from both sides now,___ from

up and down,___ and still___ some - how___ it's cloud il - lu - sions

I re - call, I re - al - ly___ don't know clouds_____

_____ at ___ all.

2. Moons and Junes and Ferris wheels, the dizzy dancing way you feel,
As every fairy tale comes real, I've looked at love that way.
But now it's just another show, you leave 'em laughing when you go,
And if you care, don't let them know, don't give yourself away.
I've looked at love from both sides now, from give and take, and still somehow
It's love's illusions I recall, I really don't know love at all.

3. Tears and fears and feeling proud, to say "I love you" right out loud,
Dreams and schemes and circus crowds, I've looked at life that way.
But now old friends are acting strange, they shake their heads, they say I've changed,
Well, something's lost but something's gained in living every day.

I've looked at life from both sides now, from { win and lose / up and down } and still somehow

It's life's illusions I recall, I really don't know life at all.

SUNDOWN

Words and Music by
GORDON LIGHTFOOT

Moderately, with a strong beat

1. I can see her ly-in' back in her sat-in dress in a

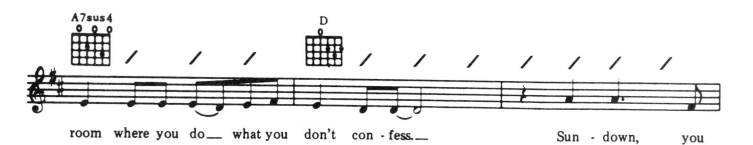

room where you do__ what you don't con-fess.__ Sun-down, you

bet-ter take care__ if I find you bin creep-in' round__ my back stairs.__

Sun-down, you bet-ter take care__ if I find you bin creep-in' round__

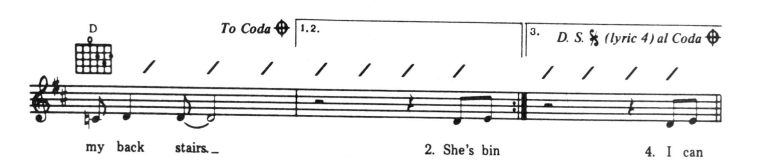

my back stairs.__   2. She's bin   4. I can

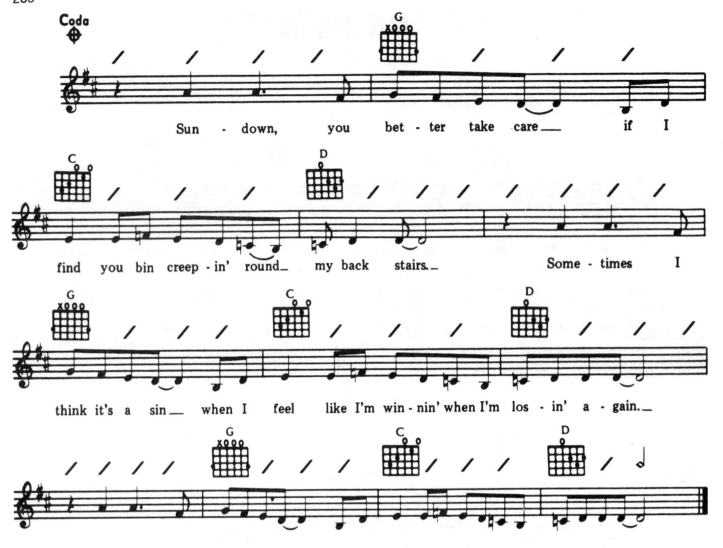

Coda

Sun - down, you bet - ter take care ___ if I find you bin creep - in' round ___ my back stairs. ___ Some - times I think it's a sin ___ when I feel like I'm win - nin' when I'm los - in' a - gain. ___

2. She's bin lookin' like a queen in a sailor's dream
   and she don't always say what she really means.
   Sometimes I think it's a shame when I get feelin' better when I'm feeling no pain.
   Sometimes I think it's a shame when I get feelin' better when I'm feeling no pain.

3. I can picture every move that a man could make;
   gettin' lost in her lovin' is your first mistake.
   Sundown, you better take care if I find you bin creepin' round my back stairs.
   Sometimes I think it's a sin when I feel like I'm winnin' when I'm losin' again.

4. I can see her lookin' fast in her faded jeans;
   she's a hard lovin' woman, got me feelin' mean.
   Sometimes I think it's a shame when I get feelin' better when I'm feelin' no pain.
   Sundown, you better take care if I find you been creepin' round my back stairs.
   Sundown, you better take care, etc.

ON THE BORDER

Words and Music by
BERNIE LEADON,
DON HENLEY and GLENN FREY

SWAYIN' TO THE MUSIC
(SLOW DANCIN')

Words and Music by
JACK TEMPCHIN

Moderately slow

1. It's late at night __ and we're all a - lone__

with just the mu - sic of the ra - di - o. No one's com-in', no one's

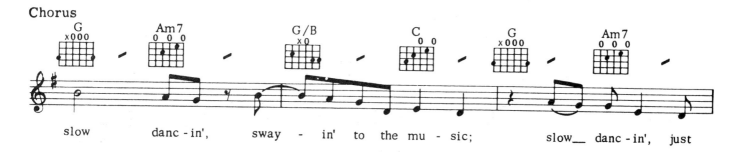

gon-na tel - e - phone; just me and her_ and the lights are low._ And we're

Chorus

slow danc - in', sway - in' to the mu - sic; slow_ danc - in', just

me and my girl._____ Slow_ danc - in', sway - in' to the mu - sic.

270

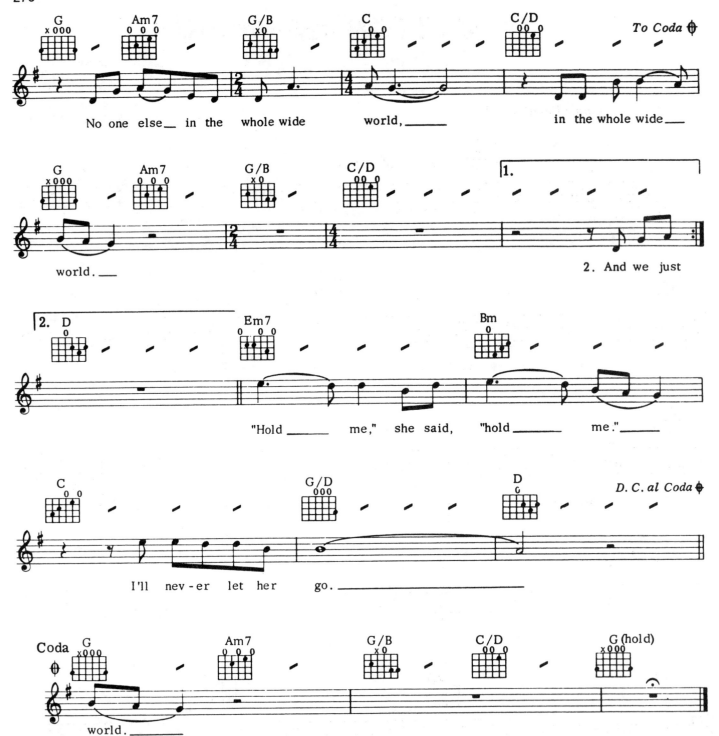

Additional lyrics

2. And we just flow together when the lights are low,
   The shadows dancing all across the wall.
   The music's playin' so soft and slow
   And the rest of the world's so far away and small when we're

   (Chorus)

3. As we dance together in the dark
   There's so much love in this heart of mine.
   She whispers to me and I hold her tight;
   She's the one I thought I'd never find. And we're

   (Chorus)

COTTON JENNY

Words and Music by
GORDON LIGHTFOOT

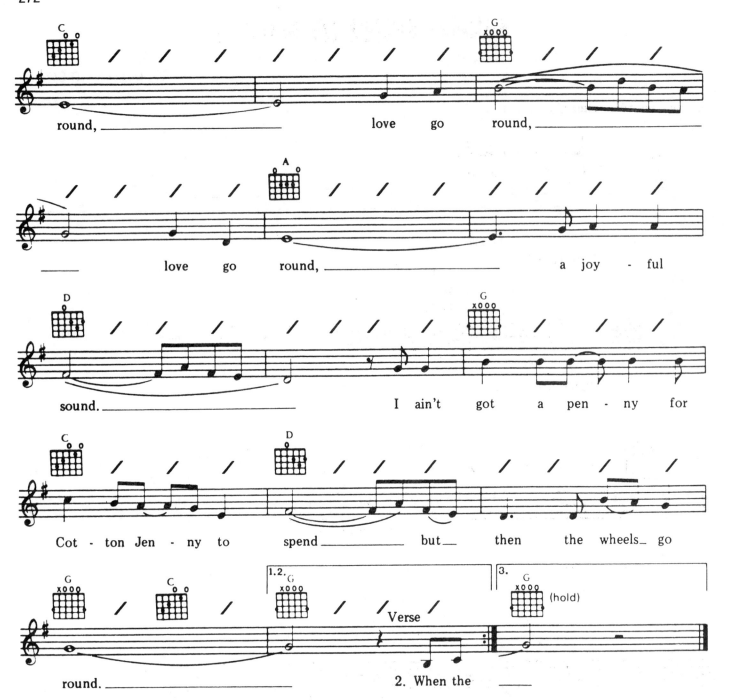

round, _____ love go round, _____ love go round, _____ a joy - ful sound. _____ I ain't got a pen - ny for Cot - ton Jen - ny to spend _____ but_ then the wheels_ go round. _____ 2. When the _____

2. When the new day begins I go down to the cotton gin
   And I make my time worthwhile to them, then I climb back up again.
   And she waits by the door, "Oh, Cotton Jenny, I'm sore."
   She rubs my feet while the sun goes down, and the wheels of love go round.
   (Chorus)

3. In the hot sickly South when they say, "Well, shut ma mouth,"
   I can never be free from the cotton grind, but I know I got what's mine.
   A soft southern flame, oh, Cotton Jenny's her name;
   She wakes me up when the sun goes down, and the wheels of love go round.
   (Chorus)

FREE MEN IN PARIS

Words and Music by
JONI MITCHELL

Suggested right hand pattern:

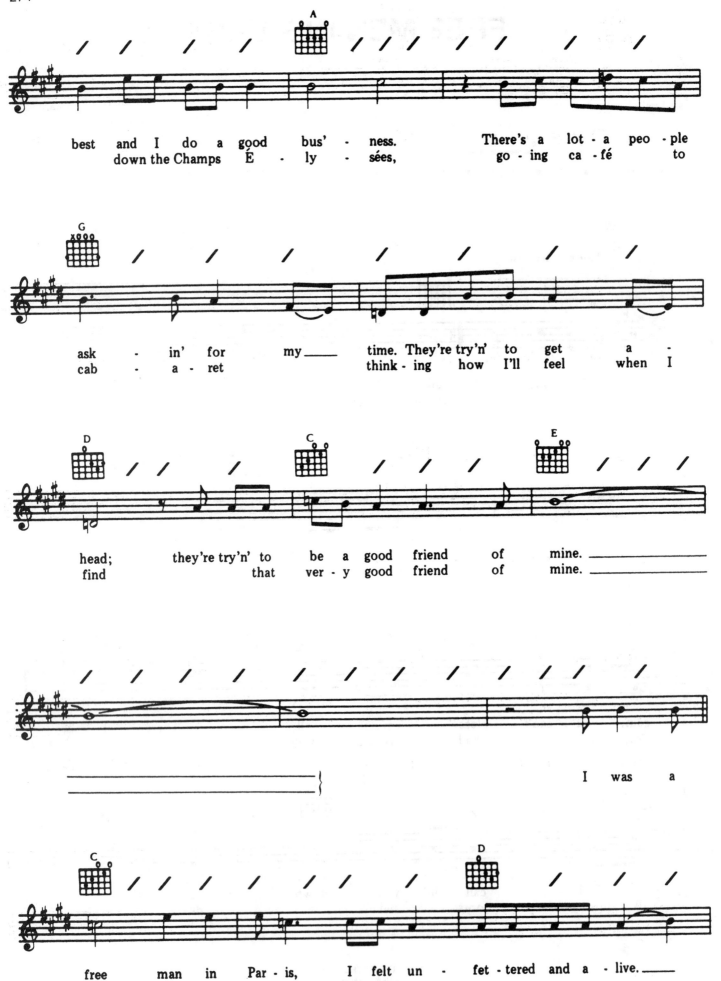

best   and   I   do   a   good   bus' - ness.   There's   a   lot - a   peo - ple
down the Champs   É   -   ly - sées,   go - ing   ca - fé   to

ask   -   in'   for   my____   time. They're try'n'   to   get   a -
cab   -   a - ret   think - ing   how   I'll   feel   when   I

head;   they're try'n'   to   be   a   good   friend   of   mine.____
find   that   ver - y   good   friend   of   mine.____

I   was   a

free   man   in   Par - is,   I   felt   un - fet - tered   and   a - live.____

There was no-bod-y call-in' me up for fa-vors and no one's

fu-ture to de-cide.____ You know, I'd go back there to

mor-row but for the work I've tak-en on,____ stok-in' the

star-mak-er ma-chin-'ry be-hind the pop-u-lar songs."____

____ "I deal in

YOU WERE ON MY MIND

Words and Music by
SYLVIA FRICKER

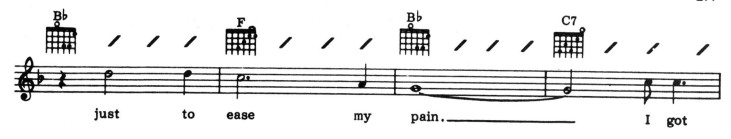

just to ease my pain._____ I got

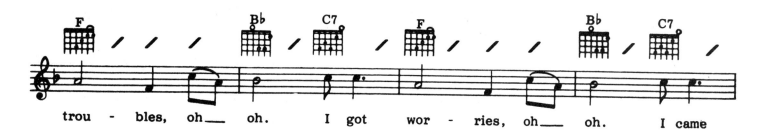

trou - bles, oh__ oh. I got wor - ries, oh__ oh. I came

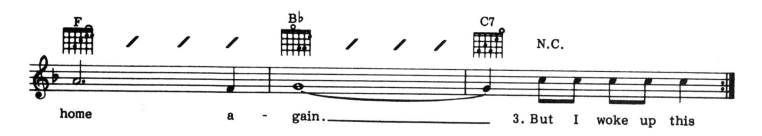

home a - gain._____ 3. But I woke up this

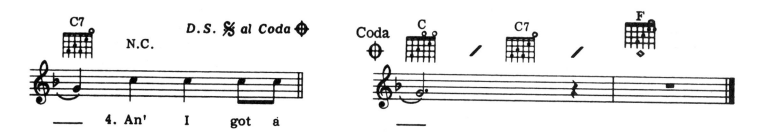

____ 4. An' I got a   Coda   ____

D.S. 𝄋 al Coda ⊕

Additional lyrics

3. But I woke up this mornin';
   You were on my mind
   And you were on my mind.
   I got troubles, oh oh.
   I got worries, oh oh.
   I got wounds to bind.

4. And I got a feelin'
   Down in my shoes;
   Said it's 'way down in my shoes.
   I got to ramble, oh, oh.
   I got to move on, oh oh.
   I got to walk away my blues.

5. When I woke up this mornin'
   You were on my mind
   And you were on my mind.
   I got troubles, oh oh.
   I got worries, oh oh.
   I got wounds to heal.

I'LL HAVE TO SAY I LOVE YOU IN A SONG

Words and Music by
JIM CROCE

279

SLOW HAND

Words and Music by
MICHAEL CLARK and JOHN BETTIS

281

282

LET'S GO

Words and Music by
RIC OCASEK

one de-sire.—
I don't want to hold her down;—
— don't want to break her crown
when she says
let's go.
I like the
night-life, ba-by.
She says
I like the
night-life, ba-by.
She says
let's go.
She's
No chord

SOLE SURVIVOR

Words and Music by
JOHN WETTON and GEOFFREY DOWNES

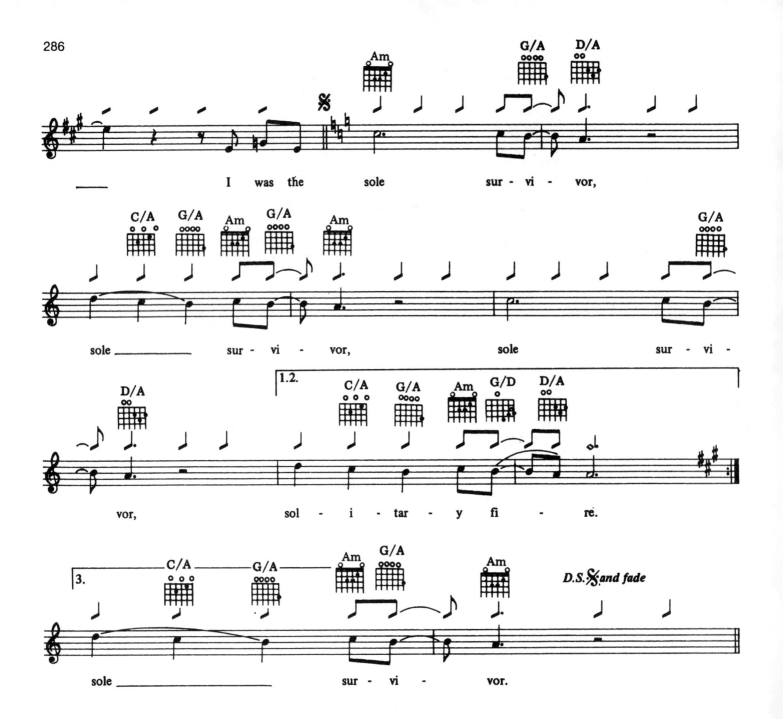

I was the sole sur - vi - vor,

sole _____ sur - vi - vor, sole sur - vi -

vor, sol - i - tar - y fi - re.

sole _____ sur - vi - vor.

D.S. 𝄋 *and fade*

2. When I saw it I was amazed.
   One-time glory right in my gaze.
   I saw the sorrow, I saw the joy.
   Light in the darkness none could destroy.
   I am the sole survivor, sole survivor, *etc.*

3. And from the wreckage I will arise,
   Cast the ashes back in their eyes.
   See the fire I will defend.
   Just keep on burnin' right to the end.
   I'll be the sole survivor, sole survivor, *etc.*